GATEWAY *to* AMERICA

GATEWAY *to* AMERICA

The Statue of Liberty, Ellis Island and Seven Other Historic Places

Gordon Bishop

Photographs by Jerzy Koss

Plexus Publishing, Inc.
Medford, New Jersey

First Printing, 2003

This edition published by:
Plexus Publishing, Inc.
143 Old Marlton Pike
Medford, NJ 08055

Copyright © 2003 by Gordon Bishop
Photographs: Copyright © 2003 by Jerzy Koss
All rights reserved.

Library of Congress Cataloging-in-Publication Data

Bishop, Gordon, 1938–
    Gateway to America : the Statue of Liberty, Ellis Island, and seven other historic places / Gordon Bishop ; photographs by Jerzy Koss.--World Trade Center memorial ed.
        p. cm.
Includes bibliographical references and index.
    ISBN 0-937548-44-8
    1. New York Region--Guidebooks. 2. Historic sites--New York Region--Guidebooks. 3. New York Region--History. I. Title.
  F128.18 .B55 2002
  971.47104'43--dc21
                                              2002009484

Printed in Hong Kong

ISBN 0-937548-44-8

Publisher: Thomas H. Hogan, Sr.
Editor-in-Chief: John B. Bryans
Managing Editor: Deborah R. Poulson
Production Director: M. Heide Dengler
Sales Manager: Pat Palatucci
Book Design: Kara Mia Jalkowski
Cover Design: Erica Pannella
Copy Editor: Pat Hadley-Miller
Proofreader: Dorothy Pike
Indexer: Kim Shigo

Dedication

To
Jeanne Turcovsky Reed Bishop,

an immigrant's daughter
and a role model mother
and teacher

Contents

Acknowledgments ix

Foreword, by Arno Penzias xi

Chapter 1
Gateway's Origins 1

Chapter 2
Statue of Liberty 13

Chapter 3
Ellis Island 41

Chapter 4
Liberty State Park 73

Chapter 5
Governors Island 97

Chapter 6
World Trade Center Memorial Chapter 113

Chapter 7
Battery Park City 127

Chapter 8
South Street Seaport 141

Chapter 9
Newport 151

Chapter 10
Gateway National Recreation Area 157

About the Author 171

About the Photographer 172

Index 175

Acknowledgments

The author is indebted to the following individuals for their help, inspiration, faith, and guidance in bringing about this historic Gateway project:

Jeanne Reed Bishop, Jennifer (Bishop) Jonathan-Caroline-Julia Spencer, Elizabeth Bishop Zusi & Matthew Madeline Zusi, Elaine & George Homcy, Judy Longo & Bill Tanko, Jan & Dave Keetley, Leo & Irene Leroux, Art & Carol Dienst, Arlene & Joel Furman, Jeanne & Joe Boehles, Monsignor Paul F. Bradley, William Marks, Mort Pye, Dr. Michael Goldfarb, Audrey & Warren Zapp, Morris-Ethel-Sam Pesin, Jerzy Koss, Charles Cummings, Robert Blackwell, George Moffitt, former New Jersey Governor Thomas H. Kean, Jeffrey Shelly, and Henry M. Rowan (Rowan University).

Foreword

The Gateway to America is more than just a place. It's a living monument to the greatest and most successful mass migration in human history. Like some 20 million other immigrants, I got my first view of America from the deck of a ship entering New York harbor. My father held me up so that I could get a better look. There she was. The statue holding up a light that everybody had talked about. Seeing it meant that we had arrived. Harbors the world over welcome entering vessels, but this one says "welcome to freedom and safety" like no other.

Stepping onto dry land meant the end of one journey and the beginning of another: becoming an American. Cynics may deride the notion of the American Dream, but those of us fortunate to have lived it know better. And America itself continues to gain from that process. The contributions of immigrants embellish every facet of culture and commerce in the world's richest and freest society.

More than just an entry point into the continent that lies behind it, the Gateway itself testifies to opportunity and its benefits in breathtaking concentration. From the creation of a $10 trillion stock market, to the invention of the hot dog, the islands that abut New Jersey and New York have sprouted successes and will continue to do so.

While readers of old-style history books might imagine Robert Fulton's steamboat to be the Hudson estuary's premier technology product, the record tells a different story. Consider the following list for example. What do antibiotics, Band-Aids, color television, light bulbs, electronic computers, lasers, motion pictures, solar cells, tranquilizers, and transistors have in common? Each one came from just that little-respected area on the "other" side of the Hudson called "suburban New Jersey."

What's your picture of the Gateway? Does "a nice place to visit perhaps, but I wouldn't want to live there," sum it up?

Many view New York and its surroundings that way. Personally, that's the way I view another place, the place that I left to come to America. As Americans, each of our lives stems from a past journey. "We are all descended from immigrants," Eleanor Roosevelt reminded her audience a mere three hundred years after her ancestors first caught sight of the Gateway to America. Most of us came later, but we all share the heritage symbolized by this unique entrance to a unique land.

Arno Penzias, Ph.D.
Nobel Laureate
Vice-President/Chief Scientist (retired)
AT&T/Bell Laboratories
Lucent Technologies
Murray Hill, New Jersey

Chapter 1

Gateway's Origins

If global explorers Giovanni da Verrazano and Henry Hudson were to sail into the New York Harbor today, they would see the most spectacular waterfront skyline in the New World: a critical mass of majestic high-risers housing the venerable Wall Street financial district ... the gleaming, futuristic Battery Park City jutting out into the Hudson River teeming with 25,000 residents and 50,000 workers ... the soaring, needle-shaped Chrysler and Empire State buildings ... the immense glassy hulk of the New York Convention Center ... the gritty, squat structures packed into the garment district ... the modern midtown edifices anchored by the promethean RCA spire at Rockefeller Center ... the nostalgically nautical South Street Seaport around the tip of Manhattan Island on the East River, and the impressive Newport Center dominating the New Jersey side of the Hudson River.

In one sweeping view from the entranceway to this Gateway to America, one can see and feel the synergy of a dynamic port city containing the densest concentration of eclectic architecture and cultures spanning three centuries of constant change and renewal ... culminating in a $15 billion marine-oriented economy of shipping, recreation, and tourism supporting more than 200,000 jobs and attracting 10 million visitors per year, with the harbor waters serving the country's largest recreational boating hub.

This Gateway to America would become the cauldron for the largest wave of human movement in recorded history when, from 1890 through 1954, more than 12 million immigrants arrived in the United States through the Port of New York, with four out of five immigrants citing Ellis Island as their point of entry. One out of four American citizens today can trace their ancestry through the ink-stained registries at the Ellis Island immigration clearinghouse.

Greeting them at the bustling shores of New York Harbor was "Miss Liberty," the inspiring statue symbolizing freedom and liberty, a gift from the people of France and erected in 1886 only a few hundred feet from the Jersey City waterfront.

This sheltered body of water and its coastal environs—which served as a vital "melting pot" of diverse cultures at the turn of the 20th century—evolved during the last Ice Age some 12,000 years ago. As the several-miles-deep glacier covering this region receded, it left behind a unique coastal configuration of tidal waters, wetlands, thick beds of gravel and silt, and jagged cliffs that came to be known as the Palisades along the New Jersey side of the Hudson River.

The main attraction for the original natives and the early settlers was the harbor itself, extending approximately seven miles, with a width of about 3.5 miles. The overall depth of the bay is generally 20 to 30 feet, with three main channels measuring 40 to 45 feet deep. The harbor has been described as a "drowned estuary penetrating landward like a pocket in the corner of a billiard table." Verrazano, the Florentine navigator, was reportedly the first to sail up the Atlantic seaboard in 1524 under the French flag, entering the harbor on April 17. Verrazano identified the major features he viewed as he made his way some three hundred miles up the coast to an incredible geological indentation found on today's maps as the New York Bight. "At the end of a hundred leagues," Verrazano's notes revealed, "[lies] a very

GATEWAY TO AMERICA
Lower Manhattan with a rising full moon, seen from Liberty Island.

agreeable situation located within two small prominent hills, in the midst of which flowed to the sea a very great river ... Within the land about half a league [is] a very beautiful lake with a circuit of about three leagues."

The "beautiful lake" Verrazano came upon is protected to the north by what is now called Brooklyn and to the south by Staten Island, Bayonne, and Jersey City.

Henry Hudson Arrives

It wasn't until 1609 when a venturesome Englishman, Henry Hudson, arrived at the shores of Sandy Hook in the outer reaches of the bay, starting the settlement of "New Netherland" by the Dutch. Hudson was recruited by the Dutch East India Company to find the uncharted "northwest passage" through which the ambitious seafaring Dutch hoped to reach the Orient by heading westward across the Atlantic. Hudson embarked from Texel, Holland, on April 6, 1609, in his 80-ton ship, *Half Moon*, with an unruly crew of some 21 men representing several nationalities. When Hudson reached the coast of Virginia, he turned north, sighting the broad mouth of the Delaware Bay and, shortly thereafter, the striking prominence of the Highlands overlooking Sandy Hook and Raritan bays in what is now the northernmost coastline of New Jersey. Hudson dropped anchor in Sandy Hook Bay on September 4. He and his crew explored the region and its native inhabitants, known as the Leni Lenape, or the "original people." Hudson's mate recorded that historic moment after the *Half Moon* came to anchor: "This day the people of the Country came aboard of us, seemingly very glad of our coming, and brought green tobacco and gave us of it for Knives and Beads."

The next day Hudson sent a small boat to check out the sandy forested area. The natives welcomed the white strangers from the strange-looking vessel, and the sailors were curiously drawn to the natives' deerskin coverings, their yellow copper pipes, their corn bread, and their piles of furs. Hudson and his crew were also impressed with the pristine landscape—"pleasant with Grasse and Flowers, and goodly Trees."

Within a few days, however, the boisterous behavior of the seamen led to the first confrontation between the New and Old Worlds. A small boat making its way around Staten Island was attacked by two large canoes filled with natives. An arrow fatally wounded John Coleman, whose body was brought back to the ship before burial on Sandy Hook.

After that incident, the crew did not want to venture ashore, remaining on the ship in the river eventually named after the famous explorer. The *Half Moon* returned home, arriving in England in early November.

The Dutch returned to establish a colony on the tip of southern Manhattan Island called New Amsterdam. Within two years after Henry Hudson's historic voyage, the Dutch began trading in furs, the beginning of commerce in the Port of New York.

A colonial government was organized in New Amsterdam in 1624. Peter Minuit, appointed director general of the new province, made his legendary bargain with the natives of Manhattan in 1626, acquiring the island for $24 worth of merchandise. The first Dutch map of the island was printed in

1639. The map was referred to as "Manatus," a Latinized corruption of the native name for the island, from which Manhattan was derived.

An English colony replaced the Dutch colony in 1664.

New York: The Nation's First Capital

The elaborate Hudson estuary, with its intricate maze of hidden coves, circuitous channels, and sandy shallows, made it possible for New York to become a world city attracting a veritable army of railroad builders linking waterways to land and opening the vast, unexplored frontier. New York would become the New World's center of commerce and finance. After the American Revolution, New York served as the capital of a new nation from 1785 to 1790.

Capitalizing on its strategic location, New York City soon developed a major port for oceangoing trade because of the availability of regularly scheduled ships carrying passengers and cargo between this growing transportation hub and European cities. New York mercantilists traded cotton shipped to New England and to Europe, while manufacturers were expanding their markets by the 1850s, utilizing a network of docks, piers, slips, and other harbor facilities on both the New York and New Jersey waterfronts.

By the 20th century North America's principal gateway for international commerce consisted of a vast freight platform joining 1,500 square miles of bays, rivers, and harbors in the greater metropolitan area. With 650 miles of waterfront, ideally suited for the docking of all types of vessels, eight separate bays were connected by deep water channels, with the main channel to the Atlantic Ocean and world markets. The magnet for this booming port operation was the huge protected anchorage in the Upper Bay by the Verrazano Bridge lining Brooklyn to Staten Island. By the 1970s, there were 400 deep-water berths providing unsurpassed terminal facilities, including the world's largest containerized shipping port on Newark Bay. Every year, more than 20,000 oceangoing vessel movements are recorded by the Port Authority of New York and New Jersey, the bistate

ELLIS ISLAND
"Old Glory" waves proudly at Ellis Island Immigration Center.

agency created to oversee the bustling activities in the Hudson/Raritan estuarine system.

Nature, War, and Peace

The Gateway to America represents a historic cycle in the discovery and development of the New World. That unique Gateway cycle was completed in three distinct phases: Nature, War, and Peace.

In and around the harbor, the natives who occupied the coastal front of this continent for more than 10,000 years lived off nature's bounty—the land, the water, and the wildlife. The natives enjoyed the protected pleasures of two little islets now known as Liberty and Ellis islands, located right off the New Jersey waterfront. The Leni Lenape could reach the small islands in their canoes or by swimming to them. Ellis, the smallest of the two, was originally three acres of sand, shells, and slush—a barren mudflat in the harbor. Liberty Island, at 12 acres, was a much larger retreat and playground for the natives. At the entranceway to the harbor is Governors Island, once the home of the largest Coast Guard base in the world. The U.S. Department of Defense decided to sell the island to private developers in 1997.

The first human occupants who enjoyed the natural resources of this bountiful land represent the first and longest period in the history of this Gateway to the New World.

The next phase was the most turbulent, as Europeans rapidly settled the region. Although the Dutch were the first settlers of the lower Hudson River area, the English never officially recognized the Dutch occupation of Manhattan Island or a sister settlement in Hudson County New Jersey, called Bergen (which became Jersey City). The county next to Hudson became Bergen County. Despite the Dutch's claim to the new territory, the King of England, Charles II, decided to give his brother, James, the Duke of York and Albany "all the land from the west side of Connecticut River to the east side of the de law Ware Bay" (Delaware). The gift from the King to his brother also included all of Long Island, Martha's Vineyard, and Nantucket, as well as part of Maine.

That transfer of land by the Crown occurred on March 22, 1664. James immediately set sail to take "possession" of his vast new estate in the wilderness, including those insignificant islands that today support two of America's most cherished national monuments.

As the Duke of York, James named his new fiefdom New York. Since the English outnumbered the Dutch ten to one, James had little concern that the Dutch would challenge his takeover. There were 100,000 English colonists in New England, Maryland, and Virginia. All of the New Netherland territory, extending northward to Albany, accounted for only 10,000 Dutch.

To make amends, however, the English and Dutch signed a treaty in 1667, the "Peace of Breda," giving New Amsterdam (New York and its environs) to the English in exchange for a colony on the north coast of South America—Surinam. Little did the Dutch know that over the next three hundred years, the "Gateway" would become the nerve center of the New World.

The Gateway islands in the bay had to be fortified and armed with the latest weapons to protect the British from attacks by any rivals. That continued during and after the American Revolution when the colonists declared war against their absentee British landlords.

Feud over Gateway Islands

After the Revolutionary War, the Gateway islands remained in dispute, with New York and New Jersey both claiming ownership. The controversy started in 1827 when New York asserted its jurisdiction over the harbor. New York based its claim on a colonial precedent. In 1691, the royal governor of colonial New York had received a grant from the British monarchy. That colonial grant recognized that New York consisted of several counties, including the three "Oyster Islands" in the harbor. The third island, not much more than a mound of sand, later disappeared in the ebb and flow of the tides, although historians suspect it might have been removed because it posed a navigational hazard.

The colonial grant issued before there was a United States government was challenged by New Jersey in 1827. A bistate study commission was created to settle the legal ownership of the Gateway islands. The state legislatures of New Jersey and New York recognized that the royal grant had some substance. In effect, it had established a "precedent." New Jersey ceded the islands to New York State, although they were only a stone's throw from the Jersey City waterfront. The treaty recognized that the islands are in New Jersey waters but that New York would retain jurisdiction—de facto jurisdiction—over them. At that time, the long-neglected islands had little or no commercial value for either state.

While the "legal address" is a New York City post office, New Jersey supplies the Gateway islands with their tap water, their sewage treatment facilities, and their electricity, without which

LIBERTY STATE PARK
Historic railroad terminal at Liberty State Park.

the national monuments attracting millions of visitors a year could not be opened to the public.

The National Park Service, which manages the Gateway monuments, views both islands and their landmark attractions as belonging to all people of the United States. They are, after all, the symbolic islands of freedom and independence.

The actual boundary dispute over the harbor waters was temporarily settled in 1899. A six-member Joint Boundary Commission of New York and New Jersey signed an agreement on December 23, 1899, along with an official map, which "finally and conclusively" defined the line separating the Empire State from the Garden State. The Joint Boundary Commission permanently defined the imaginary line on the map. The document reads: "The line now, however, marked and monumented, is absolute and definite. There can be no dispute or difference of opinion as to its location; its position at any point can be easily demonstrated as the simplest mathematical problem."

The Gateway islands fell well within New Jersey's tidal waters, although they remained under the jurisdiction of New York.

Liberty Harbor

To eliminate any further conflicts of animosity between the two states over the geographic identification of the islands, the United States Congress, in response to *Star Ledger* columnist Gordon Bishop, designated the entire body of water as "Liberty Harbor" in 1986 for the centennial celebration of the Statue of Liberty. New Jersey officials asked Congress in 1986 to rename New York Harbor, half of which lies in New Jersey, as "Liberty Harbor." That would end, once and for all, the identity conflict, since both states share half of the harbor waters. Liberty Harbor would be a permanent designation in honor of America's most popular national symbol, without glorifying either New York or New Jersey.

The word "liberty" is the common bond for all who pay homage to that special lady in the harbor. She embodies the spirit of peace and freedom and the hope for a better world for all peoples.

Realizing that Congress would not get involved in the jurisdictional bistate dispute, New Jersey, responding to Bishop's *Star Ledger* column, decided to file a lawsuit in 1993 to determine which state was the rightful owner of Ellis Island, the larger of the two Gateway islands.

On April 1, 1997, Paul R. Verkuil, a special master appointed by the U.S. Supreme Court, said that New Jersey has a legitimate claim to most of the 27.5-acre Ellis Island. The United States Supreme Court ruled on May 26, 1998 that most of Ellis Island is in New Jersey. By a 6–3 majority the court said that the "deal" brokered over the island in 1834 between New York and New Jersey ceded the original three acres of the island to New York, leaving the underwater areas around it to New Jersey. Over the years, the island was expanded and filled with dirt and rubble, growing to 27.5 acres. The decision portioned all but three of Ellis Island's 27.5 acres to New Jersey.

"The lands surrounding the original island remained the sovereign property of New Jersey when the United States added the landfill to them," the Supreme Court Justice David Souter wrote in the majority opinion. Ellis Island is only 1,300 feet from the Jersey City waterfront, and one mile from the tip of Manhattan.

The New Jersey portion has been neglected since the immigration center was closed in 1954. The 29 buildings on the southern side of the island form a blighted campus of broken windows, crumbling brick and concrete, and collapsed plaster ceilings and walls. Asbestos and lead paint chips flutter inside the buildings.

The National Park Service, which controls the island, estimates it will cost close to $300 million to fully renovate and restore the New Jersey portion of the island. Since 1982, The Statue of Liberty-Ellis Island Foundation raised all $435 million to restore the immigration center and docking facilities at Ellis Island, as well as The Statue of Liberty in the greatest public fundraising effort in the nation's history, according to Peg Zitko, the foundation's public affairs director.

Chapter 2

Statue of Liberty

Give me your tired, your poor,
Your huddled masses, yearning to breathe free,
The wretched refuse of your teeming shore.
Send these, the homeless, tempest-tost, to me,
I lift my lamp beside the golden door!

-Emma Lazarus, 1883

As the "Mother of Exiles," Miss Liberty has become a universal symbol of freedom, peace, and justice. For more than 300 years, America has been a refuge, a sanctuary for those seeking a new life, an opportunity to pursue their dreams and aspirations.

Emma Lazarus's popular poem, "The New Colossus," eloquently expresses, in powerfully moving verse, the hopes and the ideals America offered to those from disparate ethnic backgrounds who have reached its shores under often adverse conditions. The poem by the New York City-born essayist and poet (1849–1887) was inscribed on a bronze plaque placed in the pedestal of the monument in 1903.

The entire poem reads:

> *Not like the brazen giant of Greek fame,*
> *With conquering limbs astride from land to land;*
> *Here at our sea-washed, sunset gates shall stand*
> *A mighty woman with a torch, whose flame*
> *Is the imprisoned lightning, and her name*
> *Mother of Exiles. From her beacon-hand*
> *Glows world-wide welcome; her mild eyes command*
> *The air-bridged harbor that twin cities frame.*
> *"Keep, ancient lands, your storied pomp!" cries she*
> *With silent lips. "Give me your tired, your poor,*
> *Your huddled masses yearning to breathe free,*
> *The wretched refuse of your teeming shore.*
> *Send these, the homeless, tempest-tost to me.*
> *I lift my lamp beside the golden door!"*

The soaring copper sculpture towering above Liberty Island at the entrance to the Gateway to America was conceived as an idea celebrating the elusive ideal of liberty. The "father" of Miss Liberty was a prominent French legal scholar, historian, and politician by the name of Edouard Rene Lefebvre de Laboulaye. At a dinner party in 1865—the year America's Civil War ended—Laboulaye proposed the construction of a joint French–American monument celebrating the ideal of liberty. The French had befriended the American colonists during their revolution, and a new America reciprocated a few years later during the French Revolution. The common bond between both nations during their struggle for freedom was the love of liberty—to be free to fulfill one's own dreams and political freedom, too.

The Statue of Liberty was a gift from the citizens of France to all Americans. Only one condition was placed on this generous gesture to the American people. The U.S. had to provide the statue's foundation and pedestal, designed by American architect Richard Morris Hunt.

While the idea of a monument to liberty was politically appropriate between the two republican nations, Laboulaye was

STATUE OF LIBERTY

also making a virtue of necessity. He realized that a strong symbol of liberty was too inflammatory to be tolerated by the emperor within the boundaries of France. Laboulaye admired the thriving American republic, which had achieved through a revolution and a Civil War that delicate balance between liberty and stability. Laboulaye chafed under the repressive regime of Napoleon III.

Liberty Island

Laboulaye's friend, the distinguished French sculptor Frederic August Bartholdi, was handed the task of giving form and meaning to this precious ideal embodied in the word liberty. Bartholdi saw that New York Harbor, a major point of entry into America, had the right symbolic value. Bartholdi sailed to the United States in 1871 to seek support for France's liberty project and also to scout for an appropriate site for this great gift to the people of America. After checking out several places in and around New York Harbor, Bartholdi finally selected a 12-acre island in Upper New York Bay near the Jersey City waterfront, the northernmost point on the New Jersey coastline. It was known as Bedloe's Island, named after Isaac Bedloe, a New York businessman who owned the islet in the 1600s and used it as a vacation retreat. It was an ideal site because the statue would have a commanding view of the entire harbor leading to America's largest port and city. The statue wound up on the New Jersey side of the harbor because New York officials at that time saw no great benefit in having this huge statue along its waterfront.

Bartholdi originally intended the statue to serve as a lighthouse in the harbor; with kerosene lamps burning in the crown. By the time the statue was dedicated, however, electric lights were installed in the torch, shining through two rows of windows. The federal lighthouse board administered the statue from 1886 to 1902.

While Bartholdi was in America, events in France helped to make the statue a reality. Napoleon III was dethroned following the Prussians' defeat of France in 1871. Republicans and

Statue of Liberty 17

CENTENNIAL CELEBRATION
Statue of Liberty Centennial Opsail Celebration, July 4, 1986.
United States Coast Guard Eagle *leads the parade of tall ships.*

monarchists vigorously vied for the nation's soul. Laboulaye and other republicans saw the statue as the best way to establish a republican France, similar to what had taken place after the American Revolution. The plan to build the statue was publicly announced in late 1874, a few months before France was again to become a republic.

Liberty, as always, was still precarious. The republicans knew the concept would have to be indelibly impressed upon the national consciousness with a lasting image. Bartholdi, an academic sculptor, was driven by two obsessions: liberty and immensity. Inspired by ancient colossi, especially in Egypt, Bartholdi wanted his statue of Liberty to be overpowering. He also had in mind the Colossus of Rhodes when he envisioned the monument at the entrance to a harbor.

Before Liberty's appearance in the Gateway harbor, the islet had less lofty purposes. In the mid-1700s, John Bard, a physician, established New York City's first quarantine station on the island. From 1806 to 1811, a star-shaped fortification was built on the island to defend New York and New Jersey from naval attacks. The seven points of the fortification coincidentally match the seven spikes in Miss Liberty's crown, representing the rays of light of liberty shining on the seven seas and seven continents. The strategic site was later named Fort Wood after Eleazar Wood, a hero of the Battle of Fort Erie during the War of 1812 against the British.

A $400,000 Colossus

The French people raised the $400,000 to build the eye-catching colossus that would be the largest erected since ancient times. The French-American Union was established in 1875 to raise the money and oversee the revolutionary, binational project. Laboulaye served as chairman.

In 1877, the American Committee was organized in the U.S. to solicit donations to pay for the base, or pedestal, to support the towering statue draped in graceful folds of a loose robe. In her left arm, Miss Liberty cradles a tablet bearing the date of the Declaration of Independence in Roman numerals. A chain signifying tyranny (unjust rule) lies broken at her feet. Bartholdi modeled the figure's face after his mother's. The larger lady's features are immense: her nose is 4 feet, 6 inches long, her mouth 3 feet wide.

In 1881, U.S. architect Richard M. Hunt, recognized for designing magnificent mansions, was selected to fashion the massive, 154-foot-tall foundation, at the time the largest single concrete structure in the world reinforced with steel beams and covered with granite. The statue, by comparison, stands 151 feet and 1 inch high from its feet to the top of the torch when measured by Bartholdi in 1886 after it was erected on the foundation.

A total of 189 stairs and a passenger elevator enclosed in glass allow the more than 2 million visitors per year to the statue to reach the balcony circling the top of the pedestal. On the way up inside the pedestal, visitors can view a row of pillars called a colonnade.

Construction of the statue began in a Paris workshop in 1875. Bartholdi started with a small clay model, followed by three plaster models, each larger than the previous to determine the scale of the figure. The final version consisted of a sturdy wooden framework for each major section of the statue. A layer of plaster was applied over the wooden framework, forming a full-scale model for each major part of the statue. Carpenters constructed large wooden forms following the shape of the plaster model. Metal workers then placed thin sheets of copper into the wooden forms. The copper sheets were bent and hammered into the shape of the forms, a process known in France as *repousse*. When removed from the forms, the copper sheets matched the shape of the plaster model from which the wooden forms had been made.

The final product weighed 225 tons. The statue was covered with 300 sheets of copper held together with rivets, or threadless bolts. The copper skin is a mere 3/32 of an inch thick. When completed, Bartholdi's molded masterpiece stood as a glorious, albeit hollow, shell. It constituted the first ambitious half of a historic challenge for these French artisans and engineers.

Still another structure was needed to support this giant yet elegant metallic creation, officially named Liberty Enlightening the World.

Thomas Edison "Lights" Liberty's Torch

The gifted French engineer Alexandre Gustave Eiffel was given the awesome assignment of keeping the statue standing strong and upright in America's electrifying Gateway, which was just beginning to glow from the plugged-in lights of the greatest inventor of all time, Thomas Alva Edison, the "Wizard of Menlo Park" in New Jersey.

Edison's patented incandescent bulbs and electric power grid would soon light up Miss Liberty's torch, the eternal beacon of hope in the grand Gateway to America. When he first arrived in New Jersey (a full decade before Miss Liberty was erected near the waterfront), Edison set up a workshop in Jersey City.

To raise funds for the American-made pedestal, Bartholdi's torch was displayed at the Centennial Exposition in Philadelphia in 1876, attracting thousands of visitors who paid 50 cents to climb a ladder inside the arm to the balcony. The money helped pay for the balance of the construction costs of the statue and Eiffel's incredible structural support.

Eiffel designed an iron tower to which the copper skin was connected by a flexible framework of iron bars. The support system, erected outside the Paris workshop, contained a central tower of four vertical iron columns connected by horizontal and diagonal crossbeams. Iron girders leading up and out from the tower support the raised right arm. The flexible design allows the copper skin to react to wind and temperature changes without causing too much stress on the statue's heavy framework. Iron bars extend from the central pylon to stainless steel "ribs" that follow the shape of the statue's inner surface. The ribs are not rigidly attached to the copper sheets, fitting instead into special copper brackets and springs connected to the inside of the copper covering. That arrangement allows the statue to absorb the force of the strong winds often blowing across the bay. The copper skin can also expand and contract with the fluctuating temperatures. The skin thus "floats" on the pylon.

Two parallel, spiral stairways wind up through the interior of the statue to the crown on Miss Liberty's head. A small workers' elevator runs from the ground level in the base to the shoulder level of the statue. It is used only for maintenance of the statue and in emergencies.

The crown houses an observation deck with 25 windows. A visit to the crown can often mean a two- to three-hour wait and requires a 22-story climb, or 142 stairs in all. There are separate staircases for ascending and for descending. About 25 people can view the harbor and New York skyline and New Jersey vistas from the crown.

When the unprecedented project was conceived, the goal of the French-American Union was to dedicate Liberty Enlightening the World on the 100th anniversary of the Declaration of Independence—July 4, 1876. By the centennial deadline, however, Bartholdi had finished only the right hand and torch. They went on display at the Philadelphia exposition and later were exhibited in New York City before being returned to Paris. The French people finally presented the completed statue in Paris to U.S. Minister to France Levi Morton on July 4, 1884.

That same year, construction of the statue's foundation had begun but had to be halted for a lack of funds. A campaign to raise funds for the completion of the pedestal was launched in March 1885 by Joseph Pulitzer, a Hungarian immigrant and publisher of *The World*, a New York City newspaper. Those who could have afforded large contributions objected to the statue on aesthetic grounds. Ordinary citizens regarded the statue as New York's problem, or a frivolity the rich should underwrite. Pulitzer's patriotic Page One campaign raised more than $100,000 from about 121,000 contributors.

With the money to move forward, the concrete–granite pedestal was finally ready for its long-awaited and much-heralded occupant in April 1886. The price tag came to approximately $300,000. The pedestal became the home for the American Museum of Immigration, the story of America's "melting pot" in the late 19th and early 20th centuries. It was

22   Gateway to America

JERZY KOSS
Photographer Jerzy Koss, a Polish immigrant, kisses the chin of Miss Liberty.
Koss documented the complete restoration of the great lady.

moved to Ellis Island after the restoration of that landmark in the 1980s.

Coming to America

Getting the statue to America, however, posed yet another formidable task for Bartholdi. He had to disassemble his seven- to eight-story structure in Paris, pack the separate pieces in 214 wooden crates, and transport them all to the United States on the French ship *Isere*, which arrived at Bedloe's Island on June 17, 1885, after a 25-day journey from Rouen, France.

Liberty Enlightening the World was dedicated on October 26, 1886, by President Grover Cleveland, who was born not too far from Liberty Island in Caldwell, New Jersey. Members of the President's Cabinet and representatives of the French government participated. They were joined by thousands of people on both sides of the Hudson River. The harbor was filled with all kinds of boats, and the event was celebrated with a spectacular parade in New York City.

The statue was dedicated as a memorial to the alliance between the two countries whose revolutions in the latter 18th Century led to flourishing democracies that have stood the test of time.

A model of the Statue of Liberty was given to France in 1885 by U.S. citizens living in Paris. It stands on a small island in the Seine River, just downstream from the Eiffel Tower in Paris. The model is about one-fourth the size of the original statue.

Curiously, Bartholdi, an exacting craftsman, had measured the height of the monument from the base of the pedestal to the top of the torch at 305 feet and 1 inch. During the centennial restoration, the monument was remeasured. The length turned out to be 306 feet and 8 inches. The statue itself, which Bartholdi recorded at 151 feet and 1 inch, was actually 152 feet, 2 inches. The story of the statue's centennial restoration is almost as remarkable as the 15-year-long development of the original Bartholdi/Eiffel monument to freedom and friendship.

The restoration of the Statue of Liberty started out as "almost an afterthought" and, $86 million later (all private

RESTORATION
Scaffolding Miss Liberty for her Centennial Celebration. Temporary workshop is at the right side of the statue's base (the white structure with windows).

money) evolved into the most extensive overhaul of a national monument ever undertaken in the history of the United States, according to Al Frank, the waterfront reporter for *The Star-Ledger*, New Jersey's largest newspaper, which covered the day-to-day restoration activities. Schoolchildren alone had raised more than $5 million for the restoration. Private funds also fully paid for the restoration of Ellis Island, under the aegis of The Statue of Liberty-Ellis Island Foundation.

When it was decided in 1981 to go ahead with the restoration, not even a complete set of blueprints could be found. "We developed a set of blueprints that didn't exist," said Paul Emilius of West Milford, New Jersey, president of Geod Surveying & Aerial Mapping Corporation in nearby Oak Ridge.

Restoration Begins in '83

Work began in late 1983 involving laser technology and other sophisticated gear. Two million dollars worth of free-standing scaffolding went up around the statue in January 1984. But even as the outer skeleton took shape, there was only "a very preliminary, conceptual scope of work," said Eugene McGovern of Upper Saddle River, New Jersey, executive vice president of Lehrer-McGovern Inc. of New York, the statue's project construction managers.

As Frank reported in a news feature on June 29, 1986, titled "Our Fair Lady," the contractors had gotten off to a shaky trial-and-error start.

"We knew the armature bars had to be replaced, that the arm was unstable and had to be secured structurally, that the spikes in the crown had to be modified, and that new stairs were needed in the pedestal," McGovern explained.

The July 4, 1986 completion date was everyone's overriding concern. With more than 500 people working overtime, the race with the clock was on. There was no turning back. Unlike Bartholdi's protracted timetable, the restoration had to be done in three years. No excuses. No delays.

Finding a proper replacement for the corroded iron bars supporting the copper skin took six months alone. The design changes boosted the cost by 50 percent to about $3 million. Frank learned that problems like that could have been easily avoided had there been some preliminary planning.

For years, the National Park Service had been preparing for the restoration of neighboring Ellis Island, but, Frank found, the federal agency had given little thought to how well the statue had withstood almost a century of the harbor's elements.

Unlike most restorations undertaken by the Park Service, the refurbishment of the Statue of Liberty had proceeded without a Historic Resource Study.

For example, a comprehensive study would probably have suggested ways to remove the coal tar that coated the underside of the copper. Instead, it took a year of experimentation before officials came up with the idea of blasting it off with bicarbonate of soda.

All the planners and renovators had to go on was a 33-page report prepared by a group of French engineers concerned about the well-being of their beloved gift to the people of America.

LEE IACOCCA
Lee Iacocca (left), chairman of the Statue of Liberty-Ellis Island Foundation, at the Centennial Celebration of the legendary immigration complex.

The lack of preparation and funds made the mission of The Statue of Liberty-Ellis Island Foundation Inc., a nonprofit corporation, even more urgent. It ultimately raised more than $450 million for the work, an unprecedented sum for any such undertaking in the nation's history. Automaker Lee Iacocca was credited with getting the historic project off the ground and keeping it on schedule.

It was only a series of coincidences that, in May 1981, led the National Park Service to initial the first agreement for some kind of restoration work. Before that, annual inspections never turned up any major safety problems, according to David Moffitt, the National Park Superintendent of the Statue of Liberty National Monument from 1977 to 1986.

"We felt relatively comfortable in the statue's integrity," Moffitt said. "It's an exaggeration to say the statue was in danger of collapsing."

Statue Climbers

However, after two protesters climbed the statue during a 1980 demonstration, Moffitt decided the aging lady was due for a comprehensive examination on how well it had weathered more than 90 years of sunlight, rain, salty breezes from the tidal waters, and thick urban air pollution, not to mention the visible acidic droppings from the seagulls, pigeons, and other marine birds perched safely atop Miss Liberty's torch, crown, and other cozy crevices.

The 1980 protesters had used mountain climbing gear to scale the statue. Ropes had rubbed the patina, leaving marks on the statue's back. Some of the copper was also damaged when the climbers pried at seams to insert their holding grips. Although the damage itself was no more than $200, making the repairs required scaffolding costing about $80,000.

Shortly after, a group of French citizens contacted the Park Service in Washington to inquire about the statue's condition. Richard Hayden, the New York architect who worked with the group and later supervised the restoration on behalf of The Statue of Liberty-Ellis Island Foundation Inc., saw the French interest as fortuitous. In 1980, restoration had commenced on Alme Millet's "Vercingetorix," a statue located about two hours outside Paris. Although constructed about 25 years before Miss Liberty, its copper-on-armature construction was similar. Bartholdi had, from the outset, dismissed the idea of a solid statue. He first had asked engineer Eugene Emmanuel Viollet-le-Duc, who designed the armature system for "Vercingetorix," to apply the same technique to the Liberty statue. Le Duc's death in 1879 led Bartholdi to approach Eiffel, who was renowned for his long-span iron bridges.

In 1980, the French master artisan Jacques Moutard noticed corrosion on the "Vercingetorix" where the iron armature came in contact with the copper sheets. Moutard wondered how the Statue of Liberty was faring. He traveled to the U.S. in 1981 to see for himself. He presented a paper on his preliminary findings to the National Park Service, which gave its permission for further diagnostic tests. The go-ahead gave birth to the

THE WORK
An artisan reviews Miss Liberty's giant torch in a temporary workshop at the statue's base.

French-American Committee for the Restoration of the Statue of Liberty. The group included Moutard, architect-engineer Philippe Grandjean, structural engineer Pierre Tissier, and mechanical engineer Jean Levron. The first order of business was replacing more than 1,800 iron bar supports with stainless steel ones.

History was repeating itself. The French at first wanted to pay for the repairs, but as they scoured the statue's interior for signs of deterioration, they realized they did not have sufficient resources to do the job properly.

At the same, the Liberty-Ellis Foundation was being formed in 1982 as a marketing organization to raise money, coordinate events, and merchandise the historic monuments leading up to their centennial celebrations—Miss Liberty in 1986 and Ellis Island in 1992. The collaboration with the French-American Committee ended when the foundation assumed the responsibilities for fundraising and restoration of both monuments.

The restoration resulted in a bit of rivalry between the Old and New Worlds. The detailed work required in replacing the old torch, for example, could not be handled by a domestic company because there was no ready experience in this particular field. That touched off a time-consuming search that eventually settled on a French firm, Les Metalliers Champenois of Reims.

The battered old torch was removed during an elaborate ceremony on July 4, 1984. The *repousse* replacement was done in a temporary workshop built at the statue's base. The new torch was hoisted to its perch above the harbor on November 25, 1986.

French Artisans Work in Paterson, New Jersey

Reporter Frank documented the step-by-step process in a feature article headlined "Miss Liberty a labor d'amour for French artisans." Frank followed the French craftsmen from Liberty Island to a temporary workshop in a former Paterson

THE TORCH
The copper flame at the top of the giant torch restored to its original shape with gold leaf finish. Full-scale white plaster model is on the right.

warehouse. The eight craftsmen with Les Metalliers Champenois of Reims, itself only eight years old in 1986, worked out of a drafty building on Second Avenue in Paterson's Riverside Section. They began by duplicating Lady Liberty's face and left foot that would be used as exhibits in the 7,500-square-foot museum below the statue's base. It was their first job after fixing the seven rays of the statue's crown. Because the face and foot had to be finished at the same time, the artisans worked seven days a week from 7 A.M. to 7 P.M. from the first week in March of 1986 to make the July 4th deadline.

For measurements, a plaster mold made directly from the statue "was impossible," according to Pierre Rey-Millet, then 28. Instead, he and his colleagues started building a wooden model from scratch, using a process known as photogrammetry, by which computers translate three-dimensional photographs into exact measurements. Each picture encompasses an area about six inches wide. The wooden model, one-fourth the size of the original, was formed by "piling" the cross sections atop each other. Most of the time, the picture provided enough information so curves and angles could be accurately duplicated. However, fine details, like those of the eyes, nostrils, mouth, and the folds of the robe, were modeled from fiberglass prints the workers made at the statue.

The torch project was an even tougher task because the torch's railing and balcony had many embellishments that had to be fashioned individually.

The flame also presented its own problems. Superintendent Moffitt had lobbied hard for a glass flame similar to the one removed and now on exhibit in the statue's museum. The glass flame was a replacement done in the early 1900s by Gutzon Borglum, the sculptor of the Mount Rushmore National Memorial in South Dakota. The glass panels had been crafted by Edgar Bostock, a New Jersey glazier. Borglum had cut holes in the original flame and inserted ill-fitted glass that later led to extensive corrosion. Not wanting to repeat the mistakes of the past, the 1980s restorers returned to Bartholdi's original golden gilded flame. The gilding was not a modern embellishment, but a technique based on a late 19th century newspaper clipping noting that the torch had been regilded. Borglum had never seen that news clip before making his fateful glass changes to the original 3,600-pound assembly.

Up to that point, the design of the flame had been based on photos taken during the torch's 1876 fundraising tour of the United States. "We had a lot of photos from the U.S. tour, but it seems when it went back to France, they changed it," according to Philip Kleiner of Spring Valley, New York, project executive for Lehrer-McGovern. Consequently the French metal restorers, working in a shop in the historic industrial city of Paterson, had to make an 11th-hour change in their design in 1984.

The new torch and flame were re-created down to the last finite detail—a duplicate of Bartholdi's original. The new assembly was lifted to its place above Miss Liberty's right index finger on November 25, 1985. As reported by then *Star-Ledger* feature writer Anne-Marie Cottone, "the Stars and Stripes and the French Tricolor rippled in the breeze as the new 3,800-pound torch with its surrounding ornamental balcony was secured on a large metal hook and hoisted up nearly 300 feet to the tip of Lady Liberty's finger, where workmen waited to fasten it in place."

Unlike its predecessor, the new torch was not lighted from within. Instead, the 16-foot flame of copper with a gold leaf overlay was illuminated by a new lighting system from the outside.

French workers had made the balcony flooring and all the ornamental elements of the surrounding rail, including the acanthus leaves, spears, and ears of corn that adorn the balcony sides.

The Flame's 5,000 Golden Leaves

The flame's gilding was the work of Robert and Fabrice Gohard, a job that took the father-and-son team two weeks to finish. Before they started, the copper flame was coated with a primer topped by three layers of varnish. Then sizing, which acts as glue, was applied. About 5,000 squares of gold leaf, each valued at about $1, were then pressed delicately onto the treated copper surface. The tissue-thin squares were applied with a stiff brush that the Gohards first touched to their cheek or hand to remove any static electricity that would prevent the gold leafs from adhering to the surface.

For the Liberty flame, the Gohards used a "special gold" leaf. It was the first time they worked together on a project. Robert was 57 when he worked on the flame in 1985, and his son, Fabrice, was 32. Robert had been a gilder for 43 years and Fabrice for 13 years before they combined their talents to put the finishing touches to the flame. "Lady Liberty is a monument without equal," Robert remarked.

The new copper torch and flame were coated with an alkaline solution so its natural orange color would not clash with the rest of the century-old statue's green patina. If history is any guide, it should take about 20 years before the natural elements allow the torch to blend in entirely with the statue.

The crown also required an overhaul. The seven points, about nine feet in length, are made of bronze and the tops and bottoms of sheet brass. Some 1,500 screws holding the points together had to be made to replace ones improperly fitted during an earlier restoration. The 38 iron fasteners, by which the points are affixed to the statue's head, were replaced with brass ones. The faithful restorers used brass to keep it in the copper family and to prevent corrosion.

While much of the upper pieces had to be replaced, significant engineering alignment also had to be executed. The improper installation in 1886 of the torch-bearing arm—18 inches to the right and forward of the central pylon—was an error that could be remedied merely by adding a few braces to the iron skeleton.

Removal had been contemplated. But testing showed the layered composition of the puddled iron support was so soft that, rather than cause cracks, the wind movement actually caused it to reinforce itself. "Even at an accelerated rate, it should last 10,000 years because the material is so soft," predicted architect Richard Hayden.

The elaborate system is anchored to the concrete pedestal by connecting rods that are now visible to the tourists, as is the copper interior since the screening around the spiral stairs has been removed.

A Computerized Face-Lift

The statue is held in place by tension rods anchored to beams embedded in the concrete pedestal. But the bolts holding the rods "were out of tune," Hayden noted. Instead of the original wrenches (preserved in the museum) used by the workers who erected the statue, 30-ton hydraulic jacks and computerized instruments were used to tighten the bolts, each about six inches in diameter.

The engineers who worked on the statue praised Eiffel posthumously for his enduring legacy. "It was probably designed for conditions never met but once a century and it has held up," commented Edward Cohen, managing partner of Ammann & Whitney, the New York engineering consultant on the restoration project. "It survives today because of the technical genius of a civil engineer," Cohen said.

The problem with the armature, however, was something neither Eiffel nor Bartholdi could have foreseen. Originally it was thought that many of the armature bars could be preserved after a clearing and all that would be needed was a new system for keeping the iron and copper apart, Hayden explained. "We were going to leave the old armature in place and just replace the pieces that were heavily deteriorated. But then we found that 30 percent of the saddles (holding the bars in place) had failed or were in advanced state of failure."

With the exception of five bars in the statue's left foot, 1,825 armature bars had to be replaced with stainless steel ones.

A serious problem, however, was discovered shortly after the contract was awarded to two New York companies, NAB Construction and P.A. Fiebiger. When work began, it was found that the bending involved in the process caused "hard spots where the stresses built up," Kleiner said. To resolve that, an annealing process, devised by Lors Machinery, Inc. of Union, New Jersey, was introduced. It involved a machine that would electrically heat the bars to 1,900 degrees, "leveling off the stresses."

"The whole process was something that came up afterward," Kleiner related. "We also discovered that the stainless steel was getting rusty. In the handling, it was picking up impurities and rust."

34 Gateway to America

STATUE OF LIBERTY
National Park Service is guardian of Liberty Island. Pictured is Kevin Buckley, General Superintendent of Gateway National Recreation Area (1986).

Another step had to be introduced in which each bar was immersed, or "passivated," in a purifying bath of nitric acid.

The process was further prolonged because only 12 to 15 bars in four specific areas of the statue could be removed at one time so the statue would not lose its shape in the constant wind.

Also, after removal, each bar had to be washed of the asbestos that had been placed between it and the copper skin as an insulator. After that, the old bar was used to shape a template. Then the new bar was shaped, annealed, sandblasted for smoothness, and passivated overnight. Finally its back was given a Teflon coat to insulate it from the copper.

Each new bar was returned to the statue about 30 hours after the original was removed.

In all, the removal and replacement took six months to complete, not including the six months it took the contractors to devise a system compatible with the existing conditions.

The paint coating the copper had to be removed by liquid nitrogen. "Originally, the thought was to remove it all with chemicals," Kleiner said. "But using them in such a confined area would have posed safety problems for workers."

Dry ice, another method considered, also wasn't practical, Kleiner learned.

Far from being a cosmetic decision, the paint was removed because, according to Bartholdi's journal, he believed the exposed nature of the copper would make it easy to maintain.

"In regard to the preservation of the work, since all the elements of its construction are everywhere visible on the inside in all their details, it will be kept in good condition," Bartholdi wrote.

By using liquid nitrogen at a temperature of 300 degrees below zero, it took a month to remove what Kleiner estimated was some dozen layers of the green paint.

The coal tar remained and, again, not damaging the skin was a primary consideration. The underside of the skin, with its 100-year-old hammer blows, also told its own story of artisans at work. Spraying the tar with iron shot was ruled out. Also dismissed was an idea to use walnut shells, which are used to clean the interiors of oceangoing tankers. Finally, a chemist came up with the idea of using bicarbonate of soda. After barges of the stuff—donated by Arm & Hammer—were brought to the island, removing the coal took several months.

An Around-the-Clock Marathon

Because of the various delays, the confined spaces, and the danger posed by flying debris to workers below, contracts piggybacked on each other and the restoration frequently became a 24-hour-a-day, seven-day-a-week exhausting, working marathon, Frank reported.

In general, the various craft unions were cooperative, with only one day of picketing throughout the restoration. "They collected overtime; some work rules were relaxed," Kleiner disclosed. "A feeling of pride and patriotism prevailed at the job site."

Before the centennial overhaul, some repairs had been made on the statue in 1936 and again in 1976. In the 1986 project, corroded sections such as the acron at the base of the torch, slits across the statue's eyes, and a curl of its hair were patched.

"It was at least 10 years too early for a big disaster," Hayden estimated. "But it took an event, a centennial, to really focus in on the complete restoration."

No detail in the statue's restoration, even those not visible to the eye, was overlooked. A new red, white, and blue power cable was plugged into the electric service to Liberty Island on April 28, 1986. The cable, stretching 2,200 feet from the Jersey City waterfront, was put in place by workers aboard a barge. Divers buried the cable below the harbor's mud. The additional power, furnished by Public Service Electric & Gas Company—New Jersey's largest utility—was needed for a new air conditioning system and elevators within the statue, as well as the new exterior lighting system illuminating the monument and its torch. The 4,160-volt line has a rated capacity of 500 amps, replacing a 250-amp line installed in 1936. The cable carries enough electricity to serve 5,000 homes. The line was fabricated by the Okanite Company of Ramsey. Nearly five inches thick, the cable carries three conductors, as well as a fiber optics telecommunications line for future use. After its fabrication, the power cable was shipped to the Simplex Wire and Cable Company in New Hampshire, where it was wrapped by 21 strands of galvanized steel armored wire to protect the interior from damage. The cable was then coated in red, white, and blue plastic. Both companies donated materials and services to the statue's restoration.

Everything was ready for the big birthday blowout. The 22 square-rigger and three- and four-masted tall ships sailed from around the world to participate in Liberty Weekend. They were complemented by 64 medium-sized tall ships which, in turn, were part of close to 300 ships saluting the great lady in the harbor for the second back-to-back biggest birthday party ever witnessed—or recorded—in American history. The 1976 bicentennial was the first pace-setter.

A Laser-Beam Dedication

Some 4,000 persons from around the U.S. and numerous countries around the world each paid $5,000 for their seats on Governors Island on an invitation-only basis. They faced the newly refurbished Lady only 1,700 feet across the water, officially named Liberty Harbor in her honor.

Right behind the Lady, in Liberty State Park, another 250,000 people waited for the moment when the torch would once again be lit after 2.5 years of darkness.

On both sides of the Hudson River and Bay, more than a million people waited and watched for that one split second when President Ronald Reagan, shortly after dusk, touched a button that triggered a mile-long laser beam activating the brilliant new floodlights that defined Lady Liberty's features as never before. The golden flame alone requires 16 250-watt quarts lamps.

When the statue came ablaze with lights, the roar of the crowds joined with the sounding of hundreds of whistles, sirens, and horns from the flotilla of tall ships and yachts and countless smaller craft in the harbor.

The ceremonial setting, an open amphitheater that Hollywood producer David Wolper built at the southern tip of the Coast Guard installation, was a mix of pomp and Broadway.

President Reagan, a former actor and Governor of California, presided over the Liberty festivities, proclaiming that the statue "is still giving life to the dream that brought her to us." With his wife, Nancy, a former actress, at his side, President Reagan told a world watching on their television sets that "We dare to hope for our children that they will always find here the lady of liberty in a land that is free. We dare to hope, too, that we will understand that our work as Americans can never be said to be truly done—that every man, woman, and child shares in our gift, in our hope, until each of God's creatures stands with us in the light of liberty."

French President François Mitterand recalled his country's role in the American Revolution and "in return, twice you gave your blood to help us save both our independence and freedom."

The French President said, "May our children's children celebrate together 100 years from now, and in centuries to come, the joy of free men in a world of peace."

President Reagan extended a hearty "God Bless America and vive la France!"

The President was introduced by Lee Iacocca, the guiding spirit and force behind the restoration of both Miss Liberty and Ellis Island.

Among the entertainers performing were Gregory Peck, Elizabeth Taylor, Neil Diamond, Frank Sinatra, Debbie Allen, and Mikhail Baryshnikov, the Russian émigré who was one of 100 immigrants who had taken the oath of citizenship on Ellis Island earlier that day. At the birthday ceremony that evening on Governors Island, Baryshnikov danced to the music of George Gershwin. Other selections included the music of Aaron Copeland, John Philip Sousa, and Irving Berlin, who was one of 12 naturalized Americans awarded the Medal of Liberty by President Reagan.

Coretta Scott King, widow of the slain civil rights activist Martin Luther King Jr., commented: "In the nation, there are inherent contradictions in terms of what we have put forth as our ideals and what we have realized. What this occasion should stand for is that the nation will recommit itself to the ideas of freedom and justice and equality for all people."

There was something for everyone during Liberty Weekend. The main event was staged for the world to see—and a brilliant spectacle it was to behold, especially the thunderously colorful display of fireworks and the rockets red glare that rivaled America's bicentennial celebration in 1976.

Five other events throughout the weekend brought together hundreds of thousands of people from all walks of life, everywhere. The events mirrored the great American melting pot, a synthesis of different people and ideas.

One child perhaps summed up it best for everyone. Twelve-year-old Amanda Harding of Haworth, New Jersey, performed during the ceremony in "Immigrants," a song, dance, and narrative salute evoking the immigrant experience. Amanda expressed the universal feeling of those who participated and those who have been touched by Miss Liberty's values over the past century

"It means freedom and liberty, and people came to this country to be free," Amanda said, simply and eloquently.

Facts about the most recognized symbol of liberty in the world:

	Standard	**Metric**
Height from base to torch	151' 1"	46.50 m
Foundation of pedestal to torch	305' 1"	92.99 m
Heel to top of head	111' 1"	33.86 m
Length of hand	16' 5"	5.00 m
Index finger	8' 0"	2.44 m
Circumference at second joint	3' 6"	1.07 m
Size of fingernail	13" × 10"	.33 × .25 m
Head from chin to cranium	17' 3"	5.26 m
Head thickness from ear to ear	10' 0"	3.05 m
Distance across the eye	2' 6"	.76 m
Length of nose	4' 6"	1.48 m
Right arm length	42' 0"	12.80 m
Right arm greatest thickness	12' 0"	3.66 m
Thickness of waist	35' 0"	10.67 m
Width of mouth	3' 0"	.91 m
Tablet length	23' 7"	7.19 m

Tablet width	13' 7"	4.14 m
Tablet thickness	2' 0"	.61 m
Height of granite pedestal	89' 0"	27.13 m
Height of foundation	65' 0"	19.81 m
Weight of copper in statue	200,000 pounds	(100 tons)
Weight of steel in statue	250,000 pounds	(125 tons)
Total weight in statue	450,000 pounds	(225 tons)

(*Source: National Park Service*)

Bibliography

The World Book Encyclopedia, Volume 18, 1988, World Book, Inc., a Scott Fetzer company, Chicago.

The New Columbia Encyclopedia, 1975, Columbia University Press, New York.

The Encyclopedia Americana International Edition, 1989, Grolier Incorporated, Danbury, Conn.

"Statue of Liberty National Monument" (official brochure), U.S. Department of the Interior; National Park Service, New York.

"Our Fair Lady," by Al Frank, *The Sunday Star-Ledger* Newark, N.J., June 29, 1986.

"Probing a deep Oyster Islands ownership feud," by Gordon Bishop, *The Star-Ledger*, Newark, N.J., June 8, 1976.

"Statue of Liberty's home should be Liberty Harbor," Gordon Bishop's column, *The Star-Ledger*, August 14, 1985.

"Lady Liberty shines in Jersey under 1889 pact with N.Y.," by Al Frank, *The Star-Ledger*, August 11, 1985.

"Miss Liberty a labor d'amour for French artisans," by Al Frank, *The Star-Ledger*, April 27, 1986.

"Miss Liberty's torch dazzles at first look," by Al Frank, *The Star-Ledger*, November 1, 1985.

"Liberty again carries a torch for freedom," by Anne-Marie Cottone, *The Star-Ledger*, November 26, 1985.

"America launching hoopla in salute to Lady Liberty," by Al Frank, *The Star-Ledger*, July 3, 1986.

"THE LAMP OF LIBERTY," by Al Frank, *The Star-Ledger*, July 4, 1986.

"Crowd of VIPs thrills to relighting of torch," by Jason Jett, *The Star-Ledger*, July 4, 1976.

Chapter 3

Ellis Island

For some 12 million immigrants arriving with only a sack or trunkful of their life's possessions in their arms, Ellis Island was a spine-tingling sight to behold for the steerage passengers on the great ocean liners that brought them to the land of freedom and opportunity.

While Miss Liberty welcomed them with her raised hand of lighted hope, it was Ellis Island that would be their first impression of and first step into the New World. From 1892 when it opened until its closing in 1954, Ellis Island served steadfastly as America's clearinghouse for immigrants whose descendants today number nearly half of all people living in the U.S. That era represented the largest wave of immigration in the history of civilization.

Immigration has been the story of this little island since Europeans first settled in the Gateway area in the early 17th century. In 1630, the colonial governors of Nieuw (new) Amsterdam, a Dutch settlement, purchased a small 3.5-acre mudbank in the bay near the New Jersey shore from the natives for some tobacco and sundry wares and implements. The island rarely rose above the surface at high tide. The Indians called it Kioshk, or Gull Island, after the birds that were its only inhabitants. Because the barely visible islet was awash with oyster beds, the Dutch settlers simply referred to it as Oyster Island. Later, the settlers gave it another name, Bucking Island, for the "young bucks" who took their girlfriends there for picnics and romancing. The island was a forerunner of today's out-of-the-way "lovers' lane."

This tiny spit of sand then became known as Gibbet Island after a notorious pirate who was hanged there. Toward the end of the colonial period, it came into the possession of Samuel Ellis, a New York merchant and owner of a small tavern on the island catering to fishermen. That name stuck during the American Revolution and the beginning of a new nation.

Earthworks were built on Ellis Island following the "war scare" in 1794. A serious threat of war with France and Great Britain forced New York State to secure Ellis Island as part of its harbor defense system in response to France and Great Britain's interference with American trade in the West Indies. These works were part of a harbor fortification system that included Fort Wood on Bedloe's (Liberty) Island, Castle Williams and Fort Columbus on Governors Island, and the West Battery (later Castle Clinton, and now Castle Clinton National Monument) at the southeastern point of Manhattan Island. The fortifications were constructed in 1808 under the direction of Lieutenant Colonel Jonathan Williams of the War Department. A "casement Battery" and a garrison were installed, named East Gibson.

The heirs of Samuel Ellis sold the island to New York State in 1808. It was then purchased by the federal government for $10,000. With the harbor fortified and under the protection of the U.S. government, the British fleet never attempted an assault on New York City or northern New Jersey, such as the one on Baltimore in 1814.

Shortly before the War of 1812 with the British, Ellis Island was turned into an arsenal with a battery of 20 guns, a magazine, and a barracks.

In 1834, by the terms of an interstate agreement, Ellis Island and Bedloe's Island were declared to be a part of New York State even though both islands are indisputably on the New Jersey side of the main shipping channel.

In 1861, at the outset of the Civil War, Fort Gibson was dismantled and a Naval magazine was installed on Ellis Island. However, explosives only 300 yards from Jersey City's bustling waterfront railroad hubs worried Congressman Augustus A. Hardenbergh, a Democrat representing Hudson County, New Jersey. Hardenbergh proposed a resolution in 1876 to move the munitions depot from Ellis Island. The effort was renewed 14 years later by U.S. Senator John R. McPherson, also a New Jersey Democrat. McPherson reasoned the island would be appropriate as an immigration station because facilities at the tip of lower Manhattan were being overwhelmed by newcomers.

Federal Government Assumes Control

On April 11, 1890, Congress authorized the removal of the powder magazine and appropriated $75,000 to develop Ellis Island. The federal government assumed responsibility for the reception of immigrants in 1890 following a survey of New York Harbor to determine the most suitable location for an immigrant depot. Castle Garden at the lower end of Manhattan had been operated as a reception station by New York State since 1855, but it had long ceased to meet the needs of the multitudes seeking a new life in America. Governors Island and Bedloe's Island were considered, but strong objections were raised to both. The Army wanted to retain control of Governors Island, which had long been a strategic headquarters. The people of New York City objected to the station being built on Bedloe's Island because the Statue of Liberty had been dedicated there only four years earlier.

The decision was to build the new depot on Ellis Island, the first federal immigration station. Artesian wells were dug and landfill from incoming ships' ballast and the excavation materials from New York City's subway tunnels doubled the size of Ellis Island to more than six acres.

While the immigrant station was under construction, the Barge Office on the Battery at the southernmost point of Manhattan was used for immigrant reception. During its first year of operation in 1891, some 405,664 immigrants, or about 80 percent of the national total that year, were processed through the Barge Office. The Immigration Act of 1891 had ended the dual system of state-federal administration of immigration matters and established federal control of immigration by creating the Bureau of Immigration under the Department of the Treasury. The states simply were incapable of administering immigration matters. The Office of the Commissioner of Immigration for the Port of New York was established, with Colonel John Weber as the first appointee. In April 1893, Dr. Joseph Seuner, an educated German-Austrian who had been affiliated with leading German newspapers in the United States, succeeded Weber.

On January 1, 1892, the first Ellis Island immigration station —a large, undistinguished wooden pine structure—was officially opened. In addition, there were a hospital, a laundry, and a utility power plant. The total federal investment came to $500,000. It all went up in smoke on June 15, 1897 when a fire destroyed the complex.

But on that first day in 1892, three large ships were waiting to land with 700 immigrants destined for the new facility. The old brick and stone Fort Gibson and Navy magazines were converted for use as detainees' dormitories and other station purposes. In the first year, nearly 450,000 immigrants were processed on Ellis Island.

Fire Destroys Ellis Island

The fire of 1897 five years later completely consumed the pine plank structures on Ellis. Miraculously, no one perished, but most of the immigration records dating from 1855 and housed in the former Naval magazine were destroyed, leaving an irreplaceable gap in the unique American saga of immigration. Until a new fireproof station was ready, immigrants had to be processed once again at the Barge Office on the Battery.

Ellis Island was further enlarged to accommodate more and larger buildings. The present "Main Building," costing $1.5 million, was opened on December 17, 1900. An impressive French Renaissance style structure in red brick with limestone trim and four massive stone eagles, the central building was designed to process 5,000 immigrants a day. On opening day 2,251 immigrants were received for inspection. Two dormitories on the third floor held a sleeping capacity of 600 people. A bathhouse was capable of showering 8,000 immigrants a day. Over the ensuing years, additional fill was placed for hospital buildings and other structures, pushing out the island still farther.

Ellis Island experienced its peak year in 1907 when 1,004,756 immigrants were received. The new arrivals needed passports or visas, as well as manifests.

The all-time daily high reached 11,747 on April 17, 1907.

During the first decade of the new century, immigration rose to more than one million annually, with three-fourths of those numbers clearing through Ellis Island and the remaining quarter at other busy urban ports of entry, primarily along the East Coast.

Despite the waves of newcomers, legal barriers were erected during the early years of the 20th century to exclude various classes of "undesirables." A shift from northern and western Europeans to southern and eastern Europeans was becoming evident. Ellis Island became a place of trial, as well as of hope to the immigrants. Nevertheless, increasing numbers came streaming in past the Statue of Liberty surmounting the hurdles presented to them. Among the arrivals were some of America's most distinguished citizens of past and present generations.

The Isle of Tears

Ellis became known as the "Isle of Tears" for both the tears of joy for those who were accepted and tears of sadness for the 2 percent who were rejected. Ultimately a quarter-million arrivals were turned back during the 1890–1950s period for reasons ranging from poor health to political ideology.

In the main 220,000 square-foot building, the stairway climb was called the "60-second physical" because doctors and nurses were stationed at the top to single out anyone who appeared short of breath—a possible sign of tuberculosis and heart disease. Immigrants were also examined for other ailments and infectious diseases. For those detained overnight, adults slept in hammocks and children in small bunks.

In 1908, the baggage and dormitory building was completed and the capacity of the hospital was doubled. A dining-room for 1,000 at a sitting was built on the top floor of the kitchen and laundry building.

War in Europe, breaking out in August 1914, cut immigration sharply. Some 2,200 German sailors from ships confiscated in U.S. harbors when America entered the war were interned on Ellis Island for the duration of "the war to end all wars."

On July 30, 1916, explosions set off by German saboteurs at nearby Black Tom Wharf on the Jersey City waterfront severely damaged the Ellis Island buildings. The repairs resulted in a new ceiling over the Great Hall, consisting of 28,000 interlocking tiles—a barrel vault constructed by the Guastavino Brothers. A red tile floor replaced the old worn asphalt.

From 1918 to 1919, the U.S. Army and Navy took over most of Ellis Island as a way station and treatment center for returning sick and wounded American servicemen. During the war, there was a sharp decline in immigration as the numbers passing through Ellis Island decreased from 178,416 in 1915 to 28,867 in 1918.

The close of the war was accompanied by the "Red Scare," as anti-foreign fears and hatreds were transferred from German-Americans to suspected alien communists, anarchists, socialists, and radicals. Hundreds of suspected alien radicals, including the Bolsheviks, were interned at Ellis Island; many were deported under the legislation based on the principle of "guilt by association" with any organization advocating revolution.

Immigration revived quickly after World War I and threatened to reach the huge numbers of the prewar years. In 1921, a total of 560,971 immigrants passed through the now legendary Gateway to America. That year, the first Immigration Quota Law was enacted by the U.S. Congress. Percentages were established for the number of immigrants allowed entry to the U.S. from each country.

Restrictive legislation was long a subject of agitation among those who already had made it in America. The quotas were divided among those of various nationalities. The Immigration Act of 1924 further restricted immigration, reducing the annual quota to some 164,000. Under this system, Ellis Island found its importance greatly diminished. Not only were there fewer immigrants received, but their clearance was increasingly handled by the U.S. Consulates in their homelands.

The Decline of Ellis Island

The buildings on Ellis Island began to fall into disuse and disrepair. The great center with its familiar towers in the harbor came under a shadow as a place of detention for departees, particularly for detainees whose cases were being investigated.

After the stock market crash of 1929, Secretary of Labor William N. Doak led a national roundup of illegal aliens for prospective deportation and transferred many of them to Ellis Island.

During the 1930s, funds from the Public Works Administration permitted the landfill addition of recreation grounds on the northern side of the Main Building. Laborers from the Works Progress Administration (WPA) improved the landscaping and added new playgrounds and gardens on the new landfill, rounding out the island to its present size of 27.5 acres.

During World War II, Ellis Island's facilities were used by the U.S. Coast Guard to house and train recruits. After the U.S. entered the war following the bombing of Pearl Harbor on December 7, 1941, Ellis Island was used as a detention center for suspected enemy aliens and as a hospital for returning wounded servicemen.

A brief flurry of activity occurred on Ellis Island after the passage of the Internal Security Act of 1950, which excluded arriving aliens who had been members of Communist and Fascist organizations. Repairs and remodeling were performed on the buildings to accommodate detainees who numbered as many as 1,500 at one time.

As a result of the Immigration and Naturalization Act of 1952 and a liberalized detention policy, the number of detainees on Ellis Island dropped to less than 30.

In November 1954, Ellis Island, with its 40 aging structures in need of a facelift, was closed and declared excess federal property. Ellis Island came under the jurisdiction of the General Services Administration (GSA). The abandoned island was available for purchase to the highest bidder.

Touring Ellis Island on October 21, 1964, Secretary of the Interior Stewart L. Udall found the proximity of the island to the Statue of Liberty would make it a fitting national monument complementing the great lady. On May 11, 1965, in Rose Garden ceremonies on the White House lawn, President Lyndon Johnson signed Proclamation 3656, making Ellis Island a part of the Statue of Liberty National Monument. Ellis, like its sister island, came under the jurisdiction and protection of the National Park Service, keepers of the Gateway islands.

The Great Melting Pot

At the heart of the American dream is the story of immigration. One out of four Americans today (of a current national population of 260 million) came out of this great "melting pot" with its mix of nationalities from every corner of the globe, the vast majority from Europe. The U.S. Immigration and Naturalization Service can track the immigrants' movement back to 1820, when records were first kept on such matters. The National Archives houses the immigration records. They reveal when and from where the immigrants arrived at America's shores and across its borders, broken down in the following 20-year intervals:

1820–40:   750,949 immigrants from Ireland, Britain, and Germany.
1841–60:   4.31 million from Ireland, Germany, and Britain.
1861–80:   5.13 million from Germany, Scandinavia, and China.

THE VIEW
View of Miss Liberty from inside the Great Hall of Ellis Island.

MAIN ENTRANCE
*Ellis Island Main Entrance after restoration.
The ferry boat dock entrance to Ellis Island Immigration Center.*

1881–1900: 8.93 million from Italy, Austria-Hungary, and Russia.

1901–20: 14.53 million from Austria-Hungary, Italy, Russia, Turkey, Japan, and Mexico.

Post-Ellis Era:

1921–40: 4.64 million from Italy, Germany, Poland, and Canada.

1941–60: 3.55 million from Germany and Mexico.

1961–80: 7.81 million from Mexico, Cuba, Philippines, Vietnam, and Korea.

1981–88: 4.71 million from Korea, China, Vietnam, Mexico, and Central America.

1989–98: 10.2 million from Europe, the mid-East, far East, Asia, Africa, South America, Central America, People's Republic of China, Russia, and the Caribbean.

The Gateway Vision

In the late 1960s and early 1970s, three individuals played pivotal roles in forging a memorable future for the Gateway to America. Each looked at the Statue of Liberty as the centerpiece of a Gateway renaissance that would bring together the three critical components into an unforgettable historic experience: the generally neglected Miss Liberty, the forsaken Ellis Island immigration center, and the abandoned and derelict Jersey City waterfront.

A Jersey City councilman and practicing attorney, Morris Pesin, and a Jersey City housewife, Audrey Zapp, shared similar sentiments and views of how to rejuvenate this potentially remarkable Gateway to America. They were joined in their efforts by Peter Sammartino, the founder and then president and chancellor of Fairleigh Dickinson University (New Jersey), whose parents had come to America from Italy via Ellis Island.

Each set out to dramatize their case for a fulfilling Gateway experience, beginning with the revitalization of the waterfront that served as a natural backdrop to the two national monuments.

Pesin paddled around the islands in a canoe to draw attention to his cause. At first, public officials and the media dismissed Pesin as a gad-fly seeking publicity and self-aggrandizement. After all, he was a local politician running for office, and any press was better than being completely ignored.

Zapp and her husband, Warren, a veteran fireman for Western Electric Company in nearby Kearny and a decorated World War II soldier and professional photographer, approached the problem from the citizens' perspective: They photographed and documented conditions on the waterfront and the two islands and gave their detailed research to the media to launch their mission.

Sammartino sought to restore Ellis Island to its "proper place in American history." As chairman of the International Committee of the New Jersey Bicentennial Celebration Committee, Sammartino started his campaign in 1974 to resurrect Ellis Island as a great historic site.

On November 5, 1975, the National Park Service in the U.S. Interior Department appointed Sammartino national chairman of the Restore Ellis Island Committee. The effort culminated in an appropriation of $1 million, plus $500,000 annually from the Park Service when President Gerald Ford signed the Restore Ellis Island bill on January 1, 1976.

Ellis Island and Earth Day

Meanwhile, Zapp and Pesin worked with the New Jersey Department of Environmental Protection (DEP), established on Earth Day (April 22) 1970, to rescue the Jersey City waterfront from the rats, vermin, and junk that had transformed Miss Liberty's backyard into an ugly, filthy, and dangerous dump.

Pesin and the Zapps asked this writer to launch their "Liberty Park Citizens Campaign" by telling the story of the historic potential of this abandoned waterfront in Jersey City on Page One and the Editorial pages of *The Star-Ledger*, New Jersey's largest newspaper.

Their diligence and perseverance paid off when the New Jersey DEP responded to Pesin and Zapp's pleas for a spacious, green, and open "people's park" to greet Gateway visitors. Appropriately they became the "Father" and "Mother," respectively, of Liberty State Park and the new Gateway to America.

Sammartino's dream was becoming a reality as Ellis Island was opened to the public in 1976 for the first time since its closing in 1954.

An Educator—and a Journalist

This writer accompanied Sammartino during that momentous opening tour led by the National Park Service personnel on Thursday May 27, 1976. The report, with pictures, was published in *The Star-Ledger* the following day under the heading "Tourists Will View a Shrine to Immigration: Ellis Island reopening in 'original condition.'" The story that I wrote, now part of the Ellis Island archives, is reprinted in the following shortened version:

The walls are cracked and the roof leaks ... the faded paint is chipped and peeling ... windows are shattered and ivy is climbing through gaping holes ... floorboards are rotting and aging gray furniture is scattered about ... the vast hall balcony and tiled walkways and offices are deserted.

The scene is Ellis Island, 1976. Not a pretty picture, but nevertheless a major, moving chapter in the bicentennial celebration.

A huge hunk of American history, long neglected and virtually forgotten, will be recalled today when Ellis Island—the clearinghouse for more than 12 million immigrants from 1892 to 1954—opens to the public.

And it is opening in its "original condition," as restoration is being limited to safety improvements.

During a tour of the 27.5-acre island yesterday in preparation for the formal opening, members of the press were allowed to wander through the maze of cubicles and corridors where millions of Europeans, Asians, Africans, and other nationals were checked out before making America their new home.

There were no immigrants yesterday but practically everyone on the quiet, tree-shaded island was either a descendant of immigrants or whose friends were second- or third- or fourth-generation American.

The individual responsible for opening Ellis Island to the public—after it was closed and abandoned by the federal government in 1954—is Peter Sammartino, a first-generation Italian-American.

Dr. Sammartino, founder, president, and chancellor of Fairleigh Dickinson University, stood in the immigration center's main hall with his wife, Sally, and shook his head repeatedly.

"This is where my father Gaetano and my mother Eva once stood in line," Sammartino sighed. "They came here in 1900 when this

building was almost brand new. Now we've got to preserve it—for all Americans."

The three-story structure with its arched windows and elegant towers overlooking the New York Harbor and Statue of Liberty will remain in almost the same condition as Sammartino and his Restore Ellis Island Committee found it two-and-half-years ago.

"The idea is to leave it in its natural condition so tourists can see how it was—the original tiles, bricks, paint," Sammartino explained. "It would be a shame to cover everything with fresh paint and wood and metal."

The National Park Service, which is spending $1 million to get the building ready for public viewing, will welcome the first boatload of tourists at 10:45 tomorrow morning. Visitors will be able to board a boat from Liberty Island every hour between 10:45 A.M. and 3:45 P.M. The cost per person is $1.25. Each boat will be able to accommodate about 750 people, or a total of nearly 800 tourists a day, seven days a week. The island will be closed to the public from Oct. 30 until next Memorial Day.

Ellis Island is just 1,300 feet from the Jersey City waterfront and within a stone's throw of the Statue of Liberty and Liberty State Park.

Sammartino, who will be among the dignitaries at today's opening ceremonies, is trying to get the state or federal government to provide ferry service between Ellis Island and New Jersey. The original ferry that brought immigrants to the island up to 1954 is still docked beside the entranceway to the main hall. It is deteriorating and is slowly sinking. There are no funds, or plans, to restore it. Sammartino predicts that Ellis Island will become the nation's No. 1 historic attraction because one-fourth of the population "can immediately identify with it" as the gateway to America.

New York Seeks Demolition of Ellis Island

In the mid-1970s, New York proposed that Ellis Island's immigration center be demolished and replaced by a glitzy convention center for tourists' trade shows and corporate meetings. That proposal was quickly attacked by a series of articles in *The Star-Ledger*, which supported Sammartino's plan to restore the island to its former glory days during the unprecedented period of immigration at the turn of the 20th century.

For the American Bicentennial on July 4, 1976, *The Star-Ledger* published a series of articles by this writer on the story of Ellis Island, the Statue of Liberty, and Liberty State Park. The series, which ran in early June of 1976, called for direct ferry service from New Jersey to the Gateway islands. The National Park Service responded with service being inaugurated on September 7, 1976 by Circle Line Ferries and Cruises based in Manhattan.

I was aboard for the first ferry ride to Ellis Island, along with Audrey Zapp and retired Air Force Colonel Jerome McCabe, the New Jersey DEP official responsible for turning a wasted waterfront into an attractive 800-acre park for all the people of America.

A handful of passengers and a crew of three aboard the 63-year-old ferry named C. Washington Coyler made the inaugural trip from New Jersey to Ellis Island on September 7. The ride took only 12 minutes from the southernmost end of Liberty State Park. Ellis Island is off the northernmost end of the park.

The 65-foot ferry pulled alongside the rarely used coal dock on the north side of the island. During the early part of this century, coal barges unloaded their cargo at the slip, which eventually became overgrown with vegetation.

Many tourists visiting Ellis and Liberty Islands ask the Park Service tour guides, "What is that island with all the flags?" That "island" is Liberty State Park, where the flags of all 50 states fly freely in the harbor breezes.

During the first year Ellis Island was opened to the public, more than 50,000 visitors were given the 60-minute guided tours. When restoration of the buildings began in 1984, visitations had reached 70,000 a year.

The decision to refurbish the buildings, which Sammartino felt should be left as they were, was made by the people through a series of public hearings in 1976. Dr. William Hendrickson, chief of the Park Service's harbor islands operations, announced the public hearings would determine how the restoration of Ellis Island should be carried out.

Several state and national historical groups had different ideas and plans for Ellis Island, including demolition of most of the old buildings and construction of a huge "cultural center" depicting America's diverse heritage.

But rather than let a handful of special interest groups decide the fate of Ellis Island, the Park Service turned to the people for their collective decision.

"Ellis Island belongs to all the people of the United States, and we want to know what they think about any plans to change the island or to open it for year-round visitation," Hendrickson told this writer for an article published June 20, 1976. At the time, Hendrickson believed some of the remaining 31 structures on the island would have to be razed because of their advanced deterioration. "We will adopt a plan most favored by the people," Hendrickson emphasized.

The Fight over Ellis Island's Future

The two most visible and vocal groups formulating plans for Ellis Island in 1976 were Sammartino's restoration committee and the National Heritage Confederation led by Walter M. Wojcicki of Clark, New Jersey, then a senior engineer with Western Electric Company in Newark.

Sammartino wanted the immigration buildings to be left in their original condition so "the people can see the way it is" without all of the synthetic paints and modern trimmings that go along with a complete refurbishing.

Wojcicki wanted most of the buildings torn down, with the main immigration hall remaining intact. His Heritage Confederation proposed the erection of a round, Romanesque-like theater-museum called the "Heritage House to give meaning and life to the past."

Some of the buildings targeted for demolition were the ice plant, kitchen, crematory, psychopathic ward, old hospital, nurses cottage, mortuary, measles ward, isolation ward, and staff house.

What, in fact, happened was a synthesis of all public comments and suggestions leading to the creation of The Statue of Liberty-Ellis Island Foundation. In 1982, President Ronald Reagan tapped automaker extraordinare Lee Iacocca to set up the foundation that would raise funds and oversee the restoration and preservation of the two national monuments and to plan for the centennial celebrations of each.

The restoration of Ellis Island, which began in 1984, would cost close to $160 million, making it the largest restoration project of its kind in American history. Its scope was comparable to the restorations done on the Palace of Versailles in France and Leningrad's Hermitage.

The Ellis Island dream was already taking shape when *Star-Ledger* waterfront reporter Al Frank visited the immigration site in April 1986. The transition was in process, as Frank wrote in his April 20 article:

Across the ferry slip that almost bisects Ellis Island, only yards from the most historic buildings that were the first stop for 12 million of the nation's immigrants, lies what appears to be a ghost town.

In contrast to the scaffolding that marks the restoration work under way for more than a year on the northern end of the island, most of the buildings on the southern half are surrounded and sometimes even invaded by strands of overgrown forsythia and honeysuckle.

The "Great Lawn," where patients and staff took the air or played games near carefully pruned apple and pear trees, is a jungle of growth. Occasionally, a passing helicopter will frighten a pheasant from the underbrush.

Devoid of most furnishings, the 27 buildings are cluttered with debris of fallen ceilings and collapsed walls, evidence of the surrounding harbor's penetrating cold and damp.

Except for the medicine cabinet in a second-floor bathroom of the staff house, little glass survives intact. Even so, much of the copper trim on the buildings south of the ferry slip seems to have escaped the vandals who plundered the structures on the other side.

Repainting has saved the masonry on the administration building, but at the rear of the adjacent hospital, support steel has been exposed by fallen brickwork. Everywhere else is evidence of some 30 years of neglect.

Fewer than 10 percent of all the immigrants who passed through Ellis Island were taken to the southern end for treatment at the various hospital facilities, said David Moffitt, the National Park Service superintendent of the Statue of Liberty Ellis Island National Monuments.

"They were processed, put on ferries and barges, and never got over here," he said from an office in the administration building.

"The story of Ellis Island occurred for the most part in that building," Moffitt said, gesturing toward the Main Building where the Great Hall saw most immigrants lining up for cursory medical examinations and to hear inspectors ask them the dreaded 20 or so questions about their reasons for coming to the New World.

Those approved for entry were given a card with a single word: "Admitted." Those with curable illnesses were treated at the hospital across the ferry slip, while those with incurable or contagious diseases were quarantined in the special ward on the island's far side.

As part of its campaign to raise contributions for the restoration of both monuments, the foundation is raising $129.2 million for the five most historic buildings on the northern end of Ellis Island.

When Chrysler head Lee Iacocca, who chaired the foundation, was fired from the citizens advisory commission in February 1986, he said it was because of his opposition to a hotel being built on the site. He said he would like to see the area turned into an "ethnic Williamsburg" so the public could see demonstrations of how the immigrants changed the face of America.

Moffitt and other Park Service officials bridled at Iacocca's descriptions, saying they gloss over the damage the proposal Iacocca backs would cause historic structures.

Moffitt notes that Iacocca's latest proposal, devised by architect John Burgee of New York, violates conditions of historic preservation the Park Service set in 1980 when it started looking for ways to save buildings on the southern half of the island.

CENTENNIAL CELEBRATION
July 4, 1986. Ellis Island with United States Coast Guard Eagle leading the parade of tall ships celebrating the Centennial of Statue of Liberty.

The three criteria were that there would be no amusement park, that the exterior appearance of all the structures be preserved and that no new buildings be visible from the ferry slip so the facade viewed by the immigrants would always be preserved.

The view helps to orient the visitor to what the site must have meant in the immigrants' eyes, Moffitt said.

"Imagine yourself coming from a small East European village, your house had a dirt floor, and all of a sudden to be right in the middle of these massive, beautiful structures. Why it must have been awe-inspiring. My Lord, what they said about America was right!"

Moffitt said the Park Service continues to favor the plan to turn the area into an international conference center, a plan endorsed by the Interior Department in April 1983 after a competition.

The conference center proposal, which includes a 250-room hotel, was submitted by the Center for Housing Partnerships of New York and would preserve all the buildings. A similar proposal, with 300 to 800 hotel rooms, has also been made by Harvey Arfa, a New York attorney who also participated in the competition.

"An injustice has been done by describing it as a hotel," Moffitt said of the conference center proposal. "The main function is to supply meeting rooms, and lodging is a support facility. They envision something very much like Williamsburg Virginia, a place where scholars, government leaders and corporations can find an isolated space for discussions."

According to the Park Service, rehabilitating the buildings on the southern half is impossible under current budget conditions. However, under provisions of the National Historic Preservation Act, the government could lease the site to a private developer on the condition that he preserve the exterior of the buildings while rehabilitating their interiors into a private facility.

The government's share of the profits would then be dedicated to the upkeep of the public facilities on the northern end of the island.

"We are a nation of immigrants, and this is our one opportunity to tell that story and the Park Service feels it can do it efficiently and with least cost to the American taxpayer by utilizing the excess structures for revenue," Moffitt said. "To me, it seems so logical I can't understand why people think we're ogres or spitting on their ancestors' graves."

The conference center, Moffitt said, would be "a wonderful place to talk about world hunger, the refugee problem or outer space." It would also serve that function without detracting from the historic buildings and their exhibitions on the island's northern end, Moffitt said.

He emphasized that the Park Service truly understands the island's importance to the nation's heritage.

"It's not only the second Plymouth Rock, but the people who came through Ellis Island created a whole new class of citizens, the blue collar worker, and it was these people, with their blood, sweat and tears, who built the Industrial Revolution," Moffitt said. "They created what we are today and they came through Ellis Island."

Ellis Island's Centennial Birthday

Under its logo—Ellis Island, 1892–1992—The Statue of Liberty-Ellis Island Foundation, Inc. solicited funds and prepared for the 100th anniversary of the immigration center.

It took 18 months just to dry out the main building at a cost of $1.5 million. Demolition around the Great Hall cost $4.5 million; masonry, $4.4 million; plumbing, $3.1 million; and planting greenery, $1.2 million.

New copper spires for each dome of the four towers were lowered by hovering helicopters on a sunny spring day in March 1987.

The ferry that brought immigrants to the island sank in 1968 at its dock next to the main building. Repeated efforts by a Navy underwater salvage team to resurface ended each time in failure.

The "new" Ellis Island Immigration Museum, housed in the same building the immigrants came through, offers a fascinating look at the total immigrant experience by using memorable displays that feature historic artifacts and photos, interactive devices in a special section of the Main Hall, computers, and taped reminiscences of the immigrants themselves.

The three-story museum occupies 100,000 square feet of the 220,000-square-foot Main Registry Building, the most historically significant structure on Ellis Island. The museum is the major institution dedicated to the promotion, advancement, and understanding of America as a nation of immigrants. The museum houses displays and exhibits with four major themes:

- "The Peopling of America"—a graphic, colorful look at the history of immigration to America.
- "Ellis Island Processing Area"—a step-by-step view of the Ellis Island immigrant reception process.
- "Peak Immigration Years (1892–1924)"—this covers the immigrants' journey to America and the many aspects of their settlement throughout the United States.
- "Ellis Island Galleries"—these discuss the history of the island and its restoration and contain displays of actual immigrant artifacts brought from the Old World.

The Great Hall

Many of the rooms in the Main Building were restored while others were renovated to meet the needs of the museum. Half of the museum's space is devoted to telling the story of Ellis Island. The remaining areas include displays that portray the immigrant experience. The Great Hall, with its barrel-vault ceiling and clerestory windows, were restored to their 1918–1924 condition. Only 12 of the original 28,000 interlocking tiles had to be replaced during the restoration because of the good condition of the original tiles. The Great Hall will remain free of exhibits.

The museum's theme is "Reliving the Immigration Experience." When visitors disembark from the ferry at Ellis Island, they find themselves directly in front of the Main Building, standing under the recreated historic canopy—the same point where immigrants began the process toward American citizenship.

Upon entering the museum, visitors walk in the footsteps of their ancestors as they move into a glass-enclosed vestibule that opens to the Baggage Room, where distinct displays and audiovisual programs begin the re-creation of the Ellis Island experience. In this room are a visitor-orientation area and National Park Service guides who are on hand to provide museum information, organize tours, and make arrangements for the handicapped.

"The Peopling of America" exhibit includes numerous free-standing displays placing the historic Ellis Island site within the larger context of the American immigration story. Large animated charts, oversized maps and graphs, and interactive displays describe the history of American immigration over 400 years. This exhibit is located in the original 9,300-square-foot Railroad Ticket Office.

"Through America's Gate" is a 14-room major exhibit highlighting various aspects of the immigrant reception process as revealed in historic photographs, diaries, oral histories, and artifacts. Themes include the "Arrival," the "Medical Inspection," "Mental Testing," the "Board of Special Inquiry," and "Free to Land."

Visitors also see a special section, "Isle of Hope, Isle of Tears," which poignantly recounts the story of the few unfortunate immigrants—less than 2 percent of those processed—who were refused admission and sent back to their homeland.

"The Peak Immigration Years (1892–1924)" covers a variety of themes dealing with the immigrant experience. These exhibits are as timely to today's new immigrants as they were at the turn of the 20th century. Exhibits include "Leaving the

Homeland," "Across the Land," "The Closing Door," and "At Work in America."

"The Ellis Island Galleries" tell three major stories: "U.S. Government Property," the history of Ellis Island; "Treasures from Home," a collection of artifacts brought by immigrants from the old country, and "Silent Voices," the story of Ellis Island's restoration. In addition, visitors are invited to make use of two areas to further explore the subject of immigration.

Study Areas

The William Randolph Hearst Oral History Studio—a central feature of the Ellis Island museum. More than 600 taped reminiscences of immigrants are available to visitors for listening. These personal memories are a national resource dating back to the turn of the century. It is projected that the studio will eventually house the most extensive collection of oral histories of immigration in the world.

The Library for Immigration Studies—includes books, original manuscripts, photographs, and microfiche materials detailing immigration through Ellis Island, as well as general patterns of immigration in the United States. Resources in the library are available to scholars and students. In addition, the library immeasurably enhances the nature of the museum as a national institution dedicated to the promotion and advancement of America as a nation of immigrants.

Ellis Island Theater and Film—includes two theaters featuring the continuous showing of the film "Island of Hope, Island of Tears," which recounts the immigrant experience at Ellis Island through contemporary historic footage, old stills, and excellent narration. The film was produced by the Oscar-winning film company, Guggenheim Productions, Inc.

The American Immigrant Wall of Honor—Perhaps *the* focal point of the Ellis Island experience is the American Immigrant Wall of Honor. Originally, the Foundation expected the subscription would attract about 25,000 names to be engraved in the walls of a gallery in the Main Building. But as the volume of responses grew, the honor roll was moved to a 755-foot stretch of seawall that was inscribed with nearly 200,000 names at the museum's opening in September 1990. Registration reopened shortly thereafter, and an additional 300,000 names were collected. All 500,000 names to date have been inscribed on stainless steel plates affixed to a wall in a parkside setting just behind the museum.

In all, the memorial brought in more than $50 million. Each name cost the donor $100. Contributions of $1,000, $5,000, and $10,000 were accorded separate areas on the wall. Each donor received an official certificate honoring his or her ancestor.

The Wall of Honor was conceived as a way to complete the fundraising for the refurbishment of the three most historic buildings on Ellis Island.

"The wall pays tribute to all Americans, not just those who stopped at Ellis Island," Iacocca declared when announcing the fundraising project.

While searching for names, visitors enjoy a sweeping view of the Manhattan skyline on the left and the Statue of Liberty on the right.

Each name is etched in alphabetical order in spaces up to 4.5 inches long and 5.6 inches high. A computer assists visitors in finding the appropriate panel containing the name, or names, of their ancestors. Immigrants' names are entered into the computer, together with country of origin and the name of the donor.

Reflecting upon the extensive—and expensive—restoration project, Stephen Briganti, president of The Statue of Liberty-Ellis Island Foundation, remarked: "The brick and mortar that were repaired and the historic artifacts that were restored are merely symbols of our great immigrant heritage. The immigrant stories that will be told—the names and faces of the people who came to this country—their ethnic history and the emotions they felt here at Ellis Island—are the real focal points of our effort."

FERRY
Circle Line ferries passengers to Ellis Island from both New York and New Jersey waterfronts.

20 Million Contributors

More than 20 million American citizens, plus thousands of small and large private organizations and companies, have contributed to The Foundation. The sale of licensed merchandise, official books, specially minted coins, and two commemorative stamps have also produced substantial revenue for the project. More than $425 million has been raised to date for the restoration of The Statue of Liberty, Ellis Island Main Registry Building and continuing restoration work on the immigration center.

No story of Ellis Island would be complete, however, without two fitting footnotes involving an artist and a surgeon and their personal experiences long after Ellis Island outlived its usefulness as the immigration nerve center of a young and growing America.

During the restoration of the immigration center, Boston art preservationist Christy Cunningham Adams spent three years stripping layers of old plaster and paint to save old graffiti messages left to posterity and to one in particular:

"Guiseppe and Achille came to the battery the day of the 18th of May, Saturday, 1901," presumably Giuseppe or Achille wrote in Italian on a column in what had been a dining hall.

Christy Adams had wrapped the column in rice paper, gauze, and resin to preserve the surface, which was covered with drawings, poems, and signatures. Workers discovered about 400 square feet of graffiti-covered surfaces in the course of restoring the Main Registry Building.

"Some of the graffiti we have been able to decipher does reflect the panic, that despair," Mrs. Adams said.

One Italian immigrant wrote, "Damn be the day that I left my homeland and country."

Mrs. Adams found that such expressions tended to be places either where the immigrant was asked to wait or where he was detained.

Some left messages or pictures of boats, birds, people. Others simply put their hands to the wall and drew their outlines, incontestable evidence that they were there.

Mrs. Adams used the same tools to restore graffiti that she used to restore the old paintings. Chemical reactions between the lime in the walls and the salty sea air have crystallized the plaster "so the graffiti have been encapsulated in the surface of the wall," the artist learned during the tedious preservation work.

Graffiti, Mrs. Adams noted, isn't necessarily a message to anyone but the "planting, sowing your name in time."

So must Pietro Mecio have thought when he signed his name on August 31, 1901.

A Tribute to Public Health Service

The second footnote involves former U.S. Surgeon General C. Everett Koop, whose last official act in that capacity on Thursday, September 28, 1989, was to pay tribute to the members of the United States Public Health Service who served on Ellis Island.

The physicians, nurses, and related support staff came to Ellis Island in 1892, three years after President Grover Cleveland created the Commissioned Corps of the Marine Hospital Service, the predecessor to the U.S. Public Health Service, which marked its centennial in 1989. Virtually every commissioned officer of that historic melting pot era served a tour on Ellis Island. Medical training took place in the two hospitals, and graduates of Ellis Island were assigned abroad to screen emigrants prior to departure.

Pioneering work in mental hygiene and intelligence testing took place on Ellis Island, as did the development of techniques for the surgical treatment of trachoma that were later applied by the Public Health Service throughout the American south, according to Koop.

Of the roughly 900,000 immigrants who arrived annually, about 8,000 were sick or disabled and were cared for at the hospitals and in the contagious disease wards built across the ferry basin from the Main Building and its Great Hall.

Only about 1 percent were deported at the expense of the shipping company, which was responsible for its passengers' final destinations.

Captain Fitzhugh Mullan of Washington, whose history of the Public Health Service was published in 1989, reported that medical officers assigned to Ellis Island grew from six in 1892 to 25 in 1915, when immigration was nearing its peak years.

Mullan, whose paternal grandfather served 20 years as a physician on Ellis Island, wrote that the medical work was divided in three ways. Some medical personnel boarded arriving ships and examined passengers in first- and second-class for diseases like typhus, cholera, small pox, and yellow fever. Other doctors ran the island's hospitals, and the rest screened the immigrants arriving from ships on barges after traveling across the ocean in third-class and steerage.

Their exams began when, leaving the baggage room, the immigrants climbed a flight of stairs to the Great Hall. Known as the "60-second physical," doctors scrutinized the newcomers' posture and gait and looked for shortness of breath.

After that, four lines were formed and physicians examined each immigrant's scalp, face, neck, hands, gait, and general mental and physical appearance.

At the front of the room, two other physicians, using button hooks to lift the eyelids, would look for symptoms of trachoma that could lead to blindness and bar the immigrant's entry.

Any other abnormality worthy of additional investigation was noted by a chalk mark the officer made on the immigrant's clothing. A "C" meant conjunctivitis, "G" for goiter, "H" for heart, and "X" for mental defect. An "E" meant deportation.

Some 15 to 20 percent were chalked and held for further scrutiny. But, overall, the immigrants were treated with fairness and efficiency, based on Mullan's research into the Public Health Service's Ellis era.

"Their solution was a blend of science and bureaucracy," Mullan related. The principle objective was to prevent entry of someone who could become a public charge.

Sometimes the pressing crowds worked in the immigrant's favor. Kevin Buckley, the National Park Service superintendent of the Statue of Liberty-Ellis Island National Monument in 1989, recalled his mother had arrived on Ellis Island from Ireland in 1919 and had been tagged as a victim of rheumatic fever.

"I think something's wrong with your heart," the health officer insisted upon examining Buckley's mother. Fortunately, by agreeing to run around a room repeatedly, Mrs. Buckley gained entry.

Among those attending Surgeon General Koop's farewell party at Ellis Island on that September day in 1989 was Eleanor Irwin Park of Princeton, New Jersey. She worked on Ellis Island as a hospital nutritionist from 1939 to 1952, the year the hospital was finally closed.

"If you were single, you had to live on the island," Eleanor Park informed the Surgeon General and guests. "However, we didn't lack anything." She remembered playing a lot of tennis on the island's three courts and seeing many shows and movies in the auditorium.

"Even needing a ferry to come and go was wonderful until you had a foggy night," she said.

Without the U.S. health corps, Ellis Island could not have functioned and delivered the 12 million or so immigrants to the doorstep of America during its 56-year service to those seeking a new life in a new land of freedom, independence, and opportunity for all committed to this nation's ideals and values.

The new Ellis Island was officially dedicated September 9, 1990 by Iacocca, chairman emeritus of The Statue of Liberty-Ellis Foundation and Vice President Dan Quayle, during a ribbon-cutting ceremony on the steps of the great Gateway center. For the occasion, 46 immigrants took the oath of citizenship administered by Supreme Court Justice Antonin Scalia, a native of Trenton, New Jersey.

Also present at the gala opening attended by 2,000 guests were New Jersey Governor Jim Florio, whose grandfather came through Ellis Island when the building was "brand new" in 1900; Virginia Governor Doug Wilder; U.S. Senator Frank R. Lautenberg, a Democrat from New Jersey; Interior Secretary Manuel Lujan; and Jersey City Mayor Gerald McCann.

Ferry Service/Directions

Ferries to Ellis Island leave Liberty State Park off Exit 14B of the New Jersey Turnpike every hour on the hour from 9:15 A.M. to 4:30 P.M. Monday through Friday, and from 9:30 A.M. to 4:30 P.M. on weekends.

A shuttle from Ellis to Liberty Island runs daily every half hour from 10 A.M. to 4 P.M.

From Battery Park in lower Manhattan, ferries leave for Ellis Island and Liberty Island every hour on the hour from 9 A.M. to 4 P.M. weekdays, and from 9 A.M. to 5 P.M. on weekends.

The Ellis Island Museum closes at 6:30 P.M. in the summer months and 5:30 P.M. during the winter.

Bibliography

Historic Resource Study; Volume I of III, by Harland D. Unrau, Statue of Liberty-Ellis Island National Monument, New York-New Jersey, September 1984.

News releases from The Statue of Liberty-Ellis Island Foundation, Inc., 52 Vanderbilt Avenue, New York, NY, 1984–89.

Ellis Island (folder for tourists), the National Park Service, U.S. Department of the Interior; Liberty Island, New York, NY.

"Tourists Will View a Shrine to Immigration," by Gordon Bishop, *The Star-Ledger*, Newark, NJ, May 28. 1976.

"Ellis Island," a series of articles by Gordon Bishop, June 6, 7, 8, 1976, *The Star-Ledger*.

"Public hearings to weigh Ellis Island fate," by Gordon Bishop, *The Sunday Star-Ledger*, June 20, 1976.

"Direct Route To Historic Site: Jersey Launches Ellis Ferry," by Gordon Bishop, *The Star-Ledger*, September 8, 1976.

"The future ... is now," by Al Frank, *The Sunday Star-Ledger*, April 20, 1986.

"America helps itself by helping others," by James Fallows, *U.S. News & World Report*, October 23, 1989.

"Etched In Honor," by Al Frank, *The Star-Ledger*, 1988.

"Artist is restoring Ellis Island graffiti," by George P. Bayliss, The Associated Press, September 1989.

"Midwives to America," by Al Frank, *The Star-Ledger*, September 29, 1989.

"Ellis Island restoration project yearning to breathe free of budgetary woes," by Al Frank, *The Sunday Star-Ledger*, September 17, 1989.

"Reopening the Gate of America," by Richard Lacayo, reported by Daniel S. Levy/New York, *TIME*, September 17, 1990.

Chapter 4

Liberty State Park

The largest component of the Gateway to America is the 800-acre Liberty State Park, the picturesque anchor in this historic triangle. Liberty State Park is the most popular urban waterfront park in America, attracting more than 4 million visitors a year.

Long before there was an Ellis Island immigration center or a Statue of Liberty looking out over the harbor, there was a naturally protected waterfront luring the Algonquin Group of the Leni Lenape Indians to its refreshing shores and secretive coves thousands of years ago. Evidence of native encampments have been unearthed along what eventually evolved into the Jersey City waterfront in the heart of urban America.

Whether simply crossing the bay or heading for the open ocean, several different societies have utilized this special place. The first recorded ferry service to the Island of Manhattan was operated from the Jersey City waterfront by William Jensen in 1661. Jensen used a shallow draft Dutch vessel known as a periauger to haul cargo and passengers across what was rapidly developing into a thriving port. The Dutch, English, and Swedes were the first settlers along the waterfront.

During the Revolutionary War fortifications were built at Paulus Hook by the colonists to fire on enemy ships entering the harbor. The British bombarded the fortifications and took over the post between 1776 and 1783. A surprise attack by colonial forces on August 19, 1776 succeeded in recapturing the post, but only for a brief period. The British occupied the post until they evacuated New York Harbor in 1783.

After the war, manufacturing and industry spread from Jersey City to Newark and Paterson, collectively becoming the cradle of the American Industrial Revolution. Alexander Hamilton, America's first treasurer, envisioned Paterson as the first planned industrial city in the new nation. By 1836, the Morris Canal was completed from the Delaware River to its eastern terminus at the Jersey City waterfront. The canal brought coal from the anthracite mines of Pennsylvania to the metropolitan area. Much of the coal was used by the iron industry. The canal fell into disuse with the rise of the railroads and was abandoned in 1924.

Central Railroad of New Jersey

During the Civil War period, the Central Railroad of New Jersey and the Lehigh Valley Railroad wanted to build a terminal and rail yard along the Jersey City waterfront. City planners wanted the noisy railroad operations away from the populated areas, so the entire existing waterfront was pushed out into the harbor. The railroad hauled in thousands of yards of fill and created a holding area on what had been a shallow surf and lush wetlands. Such massive filling of wetlands, or what planners then referred to as "reclamation" in the name of progress, was outlawed by New Jersey in 1970.

Central Railroad of New Jersey (CRRNJ) came into being in 1849 as the result of a merger between the Elizabeth and Somerville Railroad Company (E&S) and the Somerville and Easton Railroad (S&E), originally chartered in 1831.

In 1849, Central Railroad's terminus was in Elizabeth, still an hour's journey from the Hudson River waterfront. In 1864, CRRNJ bought extensive acreage in the Communipaw section of Jersey City and opened its first terminal—a plain wooden structure. Before erecting the terminal, the underwater area was landfilled with ballast from oceangoing vessels and fill from New York City. It was the first time passengers and freight could be loaded directly from the shores of the Hudson River. By the end of the Civil War, the rail terminal provided a strategically vital link for troop and equipment transport.

By the 1880s, a larger terminal was necessary to accommodate greater demands on the land and water.

In 1889, a soaring terminal station was designed in the style of a French Renaissance Chateau by the prestigious Boston firm of Peabody and Stearns. The three-story headhouse joined a train shed covering 12 tracks and 6 platforms. This sprawling complex represented the greatest concentration of rail facilities in the New York Harbor area and of Immigrants passing through the port at the turn of the century. It consisted of a waterfront freight terminal, passenger station, storage yards, engine house, three power stations, ferryboats, barges, sheds, float bridges, and service and repair facilities.

The mammoth size of the Central Railroad terminal reflected the volume of human traffic anticipated by the opening of an immigration center only a thousand feet across the water on Ellis Island. Some two-thirds of the immigrants who passed through Ellis Island boarded trains and ferries at the Central Railroad Terminal for trips to all directions of their new home, America.

By the 1890s, the grand terminal served not only the Central but also the Baltimore and Ohio and the Reading Railroads. Major trunk rail lines ran to the southern and western parts of the United States from the seat of Hudson County, Jersey City.

Further expansion of the terminal from 1912 to 1914 included enormous sheds to house double-decked ferries, additional track and storage areas, and the largest Bush train shed ever built.

From 1890 to 1915—the peak immigration years—between 30,000 and 50,000 commuters per day were transported on some 300 trains and 200 ferryboats. Most were immigrants from northern, southern, and eastern Europe.

By 1920, New Jersey had the fifth largest population of immigrants in the United States. Many settled in New York, while others made connections to Pennsylvania, Ohio, Maryland, Illinois, Missouri, and beyond, sometimes on special immigrant trains.

More than 10 million immigrants set foot on mainland U.S. soil for the first time at the Central Railroad Terminal.

More than just a transfer point for coming and going, the terminal was an important source of employment with an impressive array of services: restaurant, bar, drugstore, barbershop, candy, and newsstands, as well as all of the traditional railroad jobs.

Amazingly, the sprawling structure was built without an architect. Its construction proceeded under the direction of Joseph O. Osgood, an engineer on the railroad's staff. The one feature praised by those in the building trades was the umbrella train-shed constructed of concrete and wire-glass, eliminating practically every one of the weaknesses of the then traditional steel arch structure. With the large skylight area, it was essential that the danger from falling glass be eliminated entirely.

The wire-glass proved indestructible during World War I when the southern area of the waterfront served as a munitions depot for the armed services. It was the site of the infamous Black Tom explosion in 1916. The thunderous blast, believed to have been an act of sabotage by the Germans, involved freight cars of munitions bound for Europe and the Allied Forces. The terminal was spared devastation because of its unique construction.

By the 1930s, railroad travel and traffic decreased due to competition from automobiles, buses, trucks, and improved roadways and crossings over and under the Hudson River between New Jersey and New York.

Despite an increase of activity during World War II, rail business steadily declined through the 1950s and 1960s. The old reliable Central Railroad finally went bankrupt in 1967 as revenues were drained away by the private auto and the new king of the road—the 18-wheeler tractor-trailer.

The Central Railroad tracks and freight storage yards were abandoned.

The Jersey City waterfront was dead, financially and physically.

Deserted and falling to ruin after 1967, the waterfront with its rotting terminal and derelict piers and rail yards were gradually acquired with state Green Acre and federal Water Conservation funds, beginning as early as 1962.

Citizen Saviors

Two residents of Jersey City, alarmed at the tragic waste of a great natural and cultural resource right behind America's most memorable monuments, became the public catalyst for action to rescue the waterfront from urban decay.

Jersey City Councilman Morris Pesin and Audrey Zapp, a housewife raising two children in a city on the wane, rallied widespread public support to transform a blighted eyesore into America's greatest urban waterfront park.

The New Jersey Department of Environmental Protection (DEP), established on Earth Day (April 22) 1970, responded to Pesin and Zapp's pleas for help in bringing life back to their long neglected, hometown immigrant/transportation shrine on the waterfront. Pesin and Zapp alone saw the incredible potential in this once thriving port desecrated by vandals, citizen apathy, and government indifference.

With the support of Page One banner-headlines in *The Star-Ledger*, New Jersey's largest newspaper founded by S.I. Newhouse Sr., a native of Bayonne bordering Jersey City, the spirited Zapp-Pesin quest to turn a doomed, hideous junkyard into a spacious "peoples park" went into high gear in 1970–71. Within five years, the trash, debris, and rusty hulks left over from a dying industrial age were cleared from the section of the waterfront directly behind the Statue of Liberty. They were supplanted by a 35-acre ready-made garden of 254 London plain trees, 166 black pines, 5,000 junipers, 5,000 bayberry shrubs, 655 autumn olive hedges, and five acres of Kentucky fescue sod. Within this instant habitat fashioned by landscape architects went 20 wooden benches, 50 redwood and concrete picnic tables, more than 100 lamp posts, 87 aluminum-spun flagpoles, an information center, rest rooms, first aid shelter ... and a family of geese that's made the park its permanent home. The trees, shrubs, recreational amenities, and wetlands wildlife replaced 70 truckloads of typical urban waste: stolen cars, shacks, rotting boats, rusty appliances, bottles, cans, and plastic throwaways.

The combined commitment of Jersey City and the State of New Jersey—local and state governments working together in a common vision—gave birth to Liberty State Park, which today serves as the resplendent green backdrop to the Gateway to America. This 700-acre stretch of valuable open space figured prominently in the story of America's "melting pot"—the melodious land of "the brave and the free."

The $200 million investment in the waterfront park includes some $45 million for a green expanse with meandering paths, a wildflower meadow, and a gently sloping Crescent Lawn for picnickers and recreation. A $2.5 million waterfront plaza and fountain at Liberty Walk's midpoint within the great Crescent Lawn are a fitting backdrop to the Gateway islands. Bisecting the park is Freedom Way, lined with the flags from all 50 states. On the fringes of the open land are trees and shrubs surrounding the Waterfront Plaza and fountain. The fountain is at the center of a circular plaza, 120 feet in diameter, with benches. In the middle is a shell of green granite rising some six feet. Jets shoot water 50 feet into the air. The water splashes down onto the green shell and into a recirculating slot. The plaza is at the center of an axis that stretches from the Statue of Liberty at the park's northwest corner.

Guiding the exquisite and timely fashioning of Liberty State Park into a unique urban oasis was a retired Air Force colonel, Jerome McCabe. He served throughout the 1970s, 1980s, and into the 1990s as the project manager of Liberty State Park for the New Jersey Department of Environmental Protection (DEP). It was and continues to be a grueling bureaucratic marathon and often times thankless assignment under eight Governors representing both parties—Democrat Richard J. Hughes (1961–69), Republican William Cahill (1969–73), Democrat Brendan Byrne (1974–81), Republican Thomas

Kean (1982–1990), Democrat James Florio (1990–94), Republican Christine Todd Whitman (1994–2000), and Democrat James McGreevey (2000–present).

It was Whitman, however, the state's first woman Governor, who finally excluded the golf course from the Liberty State Park master plan, a victory for Audrey Zapp and Morris Pesin, who died before Whitman made her decision not to fill the heart of the park with a golf course that would exclude anyone who doesn't play golf and who must pay a $35 fee for that privilege.

The acquisition of the waterfront from city to state property began, a few acres at a time, under New Jersey Governor Richard J. Hughes in 1962.

Under Colonel McCabe's careful and unrelenting direction, the first and most critical phase of Liberty State Park was ready for America's bicentennial celebration in 1976. Three years later, Ronald Reagan launched his successful Presidential election campaign from a platform in Liberty Park, with nearby Miss Liberty towering over the candidate wearing a white shirt with his sleeves rolled up and talking about America as a nation of immigrants who worked to make the "American Dream" come true.

Liberty Park Dedicated

The dedication of Liberty Park was appropriately held on Flag Day, June 14, 1976, three weeks before America's 200th anniversary of the Declaration of Independence.

This writer covered that historic dedication for *The Star-Ledger*. My Page One feature report is reprinted in its entirety as follows:

The 'Gateway' opens on Liberty Park ...

The Statue of Liberty welcomed a new neighbor to the Jersey City waterfront yesterday—Liberty State Park.

Amid the flutter of 83 colorful flags and the buzzing of beelike helicopters over New York Harbor, Liberty State Park was officially dedicated at 12 A.M. by Governor Brendan T. Byrne.

The opening of the first portion of the 800-acre urban recreation area was the culmination of 14 years of planning, massive cleanups and $1.5 million in public funds.

It began in 1962 under former Governor Richard J. Hughes' Administration and will continue for another decade (work will continue into the 21st Century), as the entire waterfront is eventually transformed from a sprawling junkyard to a veritable marine garden facing the "Gateway to America."

"This site is steeped in the history of New Jersey and nation," Byrne told more than 500 persons invited to the dedication ceremonies, including many federal, state and local officials.

"It is the appropriate background for two of our country's most revered monuments—Ellis Island and the Statue of Liberty."

Looking over 35 acres of trees, shrubs, grass and winding walkways, Byrne observed:

"Today, surrounded by young blades of grass and newly planted trees, we remind ourselves that beauty is an inherent quality in our life."

Then, as 15 huge American flags were hoisted as high as Miss Liberty's torch, Byrne declared:

"With profound pride, I dedicate Liberty Park to the heritage which ordained this site as the gateway to our nation. With profound gratitude, I applaud the efforts and vision of those persons who have made Liberty Park a reality."

New Jersey Environmental Commissioner David J. Bardin, who made Liberty Park his top priority, noted the park will replace a two-mile-long "blighted waterfront."

Liberty Park will contain, when completed, a crescent-shaped harbor-front "willow walk" ... a series of green lawns ... a "serpentine waterway"... a wildlife habitat ... a marina and boating facilities ... a restored and re-used historic railroad terminal and museum ... a hotel complex, shops, restaurants, fountains and other cultural amenities.

Among the guests sharing the platform with Byrne and Bardin were former Governor Robert B. Meyner, chairman of the New Jersey Bicentennial Committee; Assembly Speaker Joseph A. LeFante of Bayonne; Community Affairs Commissioner Patricia Q. Sheehan; Rep. Robert A. Roe (D-8th Dist), former state conservation and economic development commissioner; Jersey City Mayor Paul T. Jordan; several assemblymen and county freeholders; and Mrs. Byrne.

Exhibits of the historic harbor were featured in the park's pavilion.

State and federal officials were flown into the area by helicopter. During the ceremonies, a huge helicopter circled directly over the park, prompting Byrne to remark that the "noise is provided by the Port Authority, which is entitled to equal time, but not this much."

Finally the PA helicopter returned to its base across the river in New York City.

About 50 students from Jersey City's School No. 34 sang "Give Me Your Tired, Your Poor," the famous inscription on the Statue of Liberty written by Emma Lazarus in 1883. The Sixth Grade Chorale, directed by Salvatore Lombardo, also sang "You're a Grand Old Flag," "God Bless America" and "Preamble."

The 19th United States Army Band at Ft. Dix played the "Star Spangled Banner." Members of the band, dressed like soldiers of the American Revolution, paraded before the assemblage.

The flag raising was executed by Jersey City Girl and Boy Scouts.

The Halfpenny Players of Kearny performed selections from "Jerz," based on Jersey history.

Commissioner Bardin, who presided as master of ceremonies, predicted Liberty Park will be to the 20th Century what Central Park was for the 19th Century—a "recreational landmark."

Liberty Park will be operated and maintained by the bureau of parks in the Department of Environmental Protection.

Curiously, two persons excluded from the official program but who were present at the dedication ceremonies were Morris Pesin and Audrey Zapp, without whom the waterfront's future would have remained in political, bureaucratic limbo.

As the most popular park in New Jersey, attracting more than two million visitors a year, Liberty State Park features several points of interest, starting with the restored Central Railroad Terminal. Architecturally, it is a stunning masterpiece displaying the critical interface of America's land-and-water transportation at its zenith when trains and boats were the main means of moving people and cargo.

To the northeast of the terminal is a grid-patterned, paved area of brick with concrete bands and concrete bollards, and a circular wooden deck with railing. Yews are planted in some of the gridded blocks. Audrey Zapp Drive is the single access road leading from the southern end of Liberty Park to the restored rail terminal to the north. On the north shore is the Circle Line Ferry dock serving tourists going to the Statue of Liberty. Views of Manhattan Island are spectacular from the area north of the terminal.

Liberation Monument

Standing just 600 yards from the Statue of Liberty is another stirring monument to freedom. Created by New York sculptor Natan Rappaport, a Polish immigrant, Liberation Monument rises 15 feet high on a two-and-a-half foot pedestal of dark gray Vermont granite. The two-ton bronze-and-steel statue portrays an American soldier carrying a concentration camp survivor to freedom.

Liberty State Park 83

LIBERTY STATE PARK
Liberation Monument at sunset. Sculpted by Natan Rappaport. Midtown Manhattan, with the Empire State Building in the background across the Hudson River.

In dedicating the towering figure on Memorial Day, May 30, 1985, New Jersey Governor Thomas Kean noted that the soldier carried no gun but was gentle and compassionate and used his strength to carry a victim of the World War II concentration camps.

Rappaport described his work as "a symbol of compassion." For the Warsaw native, "The image of the American people stands for law righteousness and caring. And this is a tribute to the liberator: The American people."

Upon completing the sculpture at the Tallix Foundry in Peekskill, New York, in February 1985, Rappaport said, "Forty years ago, Europe was one big concentration camp. If America had not come, Europe would still be that today."

In 1936, Rappaport won a contest in Warsaw with a sculpture concerning tennis. The government wanted to send it to the Olympics in Berlin. Rappaport refused to have his statue used for that purpose, especially since Adolf Hitler wanted to prove the superiority of what he called the Aryan race. An African-American Olympian runner named Jesse Owens quickly dispelled any notions of Teutonic supremacy.

Rappaport's tennis work was destroyed during the war. But he gained international prominence in 1948 when he completed another massive piece commemorating the Warsaw ghetto uprising five years earlier. The sculpture is in Warsaw.

In 1982, a Rappaport piece was dedicated at the Temple Shalom in Plainfield, New Jersey. Nicknamed "Flame," the 9-foot bronze relief depicted people emerging from the flames of the Holocaust. Governor Kean attended the dedication and was impressed with Rappaport's work. The Governor later visited the artist's studio. He saw a sketch of Liberation, another Rappaport project in progress. Kean felt it belonged in Arlington National Cemetery, but Rappaport wanted it in front of a school. The story that the Liberation Monument represented was for the children and their children as a perpetual reminder of what had happened during World War II. Rappaport also wanted everyone to remember America's historic role in the ever-vigilant quest for liberation and freedom.

Kean contacted David Kotok, a Vineland, New Jersey, investment counselor. Kotok called Rappaport, and the Liberty Park Monument Committee was established with the help of Luna Kaufman of Watchung, New Jersey. Kaufman had seen Rappaport's 22-foot memorial to the Jewish freedom fighters in the Warsaw Uprising of 1943. A survivor of a labor camp near Leipzig, Kaufman vowed to meet the sculptor. When she did, she commissioned the commemorative sculpture for Plainfield.

At the Liberation dedication, Kean told the crowd of 3,000 that "this monument says, for all time, that we, as a collective people, stand for freedom and we, as Americans, are not and never will be oppressors and we, as Americans, will never go to war for the purpose of conquest but will fight to preserve the very important things that are precious to this democracy."

The Liberty Park Monument Committee raised more than $1 million for the Liberation statue.

Rappaport also came up with the idea of burying a time capsule in Liberty State Park. The capsule was lowered in the ground on April 9, 1985 by Jersey City Mayor Gerald McCann, Kaufman, and Kotok. In it were random remnants of World War II: some sand collected from Utah Beach at Normandy at the height of the allied invasion in 1944—the contribution by then 60-year-old Clement Piscitello, a retired textile executive from Clifton ... a sleeve of a dress worn by a prisoner in a Nazi concentration camp ... a letter written by an American soldier who liberated a concentration camp: "One old Polish or Russian woman about 50 came to me crying great big tears and handed me a crushed tulip ... They were quartered in dirty wooden barracks and their hospital was an even dirtier wood barracks with straw beds. Across the way was a beautiful German army hospital perfectly equipped" ... another letter by a man enslaved in the Buchewald Concentration Camp, translated from Polish ... and a sculptor's tool—a wooden handle with steel wire on both ends, used to smooth and remove clay from the clay model of the Liberation Monument.

Liberty Park Environmental Education Center

In 1986, another addition to the park drew attention from around the country. It is the creation of the renowned Princeton architect/artist, Michael Graves. His $1.3 million Liberty State Park Environmental Education Center is an external expression of America's melting pot experience.

I reviewed the Graves's architectural award-winning contribution to Liberty Park in July 1986 for the feature cover section of *The Star-Ledger*, reprinted here in a shortened version:

It stands like a silent sentinel behind the Statue of Liberty, rising out of a serene salt marsh like a medieval apparition or futuristic alien, depending on your visual orientation.

When visitors to Liberty State Park on the Jersey City waterfront discover what appears to be a fortress-like facade facing the famed

EDUCATION CENTER
Liberty State Park Environmental Education Center,
designed by Princeton architect Michael Graves.

lady in the harbor, their immediate reaction invariably is, "what is this place?"

This modern edifice resembling a Romanesque cathedral at first seems eerily misplaced, an elongated building with stark pillars and winged peaks jutting out as if trying to touch Miss Liberty's flaming torch.

Bathed in soft earth tones, the beige-stuccoed structure with terra-cotta-tiled roof and thick redwood timber should blend naturally into the urban waterfront environment. But its beguiling form attracts the eye and confounds the imagination simply because there is nothing quite like it anywhere.

Tiny square windows peek out from the landward side, suggesting a Revolutionary War fort with militia ready to stick their muskets through the small openings to protect the garrison.

The waterfront site was, coincidentally, the scene of an early battle in the American Revolution.

An arch-capped entranceway greets visitors on the one end, while a miniature high-rise condominium sitting on a two-story steel pole at the other end serves as a three-level, multi-family home for purple martins.

Birds and wildlife are what this one-of-a-kind building is supposed to be all about.

Well, almost.

Conceptually, this architectural monument in the heart of the "Gateway to America" inauspiciously took shape on the drawing boards as an environmental education center, but evolved, along with the building's eclectic design, into an innovative interpretive center.

Both the building and its purpose require an extensive interpretation for visitors to understand the full meaning of the Gateway experience.

Against a historic background, Princeton architect Michael Graves conceived and shaped the Liberty State Park Interpretive Center into a distinctive "statement" of America's hybrid development—the "melting pot," a profusion of nationalistics that passed through the Gateway and forged a new society.

What eventually materialized on Graves' sketchpad was a truly original American creation reflecting the old and new worlds, a melding of the two into one bold, individualistic identity. It all comes together in a configuration apparently meant to complement the revered statue and all she represents.

The interpretive center is certainly a reflection of the controversial artist with his own cult following at Princeton University and other centers of architecture and design. Graves is regarded as the Frank Lloyd Wright of today's generation of reality interpreters, expressing their own visions of art and life.

Graves' interpretive center with its high ceilings and cozy rooms, including an off-Broadway size theater auditorium, gives the illusion of being much bigger than its actual dimensions. The interior floor space is about the size of your standard mansion—4,810 square feet.

The 840-square-foot auditorium features a compact stage and a pitched ceiling high enough to hang extra-long flags. There are three galleries (1,580 square feet) surrounding the lobby/reception/exhibition area (400 square feet), a corridor exhibition room (200 square feet), a meeting room and administration/exhibition workroom (each more than 500 square feet), plus lavatories and storage space.

A guest book is spread open on the top of a glass display case in the lobby. Visitors are asked to sign in and make any comments. There are names and addresses from several states and nations around the

EDUCATION CENTER
View of Statue of Liberty through the entrance gate to the Liberty State Park Environmental Education Center, designed by Princeton architect Michael Graves.

world. Comments are written in the native language. A Dutchman, for example, put down "erg mooi" after his name, which means "very beautiful."

Typical responses range from "very impressive" and "very interesting" to "a moving experience" and "very exciting."

Most visitors write in a one-word reaction: "Super!" ... "Marvelous." ... "Incredible." ... "Beautiful." ... "Splendid" ... and similar superlatives.

Several entries were thoughtful and precise. One person wrote: "Very educational and entertaining. Healthy and wonderful for nature loving people like me."

Another penned, "I am glad to see this preservation—nice work."

A Staten Island man, Steven Baron, inscribed "Better than NY."

A woman found the area presented a "lovely view" of the statue and harbor.

A Minneapolis resident reduced it all to "Ahhh ... America!"

One visitor succinctly summed up the Gateway experience in one line: "Good to see what the past was and the future to be."

Some commented on the building itself: "Interesting architecture." "Bizarre!"

Managing the interpretive center is state park ranger, Frank Gallagher, 30, of Vernon Township, Sussex County. Gallagher said visitors don't quite know what to make of the center when they walk in.

"Some think it's an Oriental palace with its mix of squares and circles," Gallagher said. "Some think it's a church or a cathedral. They really don't know what to expect."

Gallagher, who grew up next to Liberty State Park in Bayonne, understands first-hand the task the architect confronted in creating a theme center for nearly four centuries of waterfront activities.

"It is difficult to mesh historical and natural sciences developments into one building and not come out looking somewhat like a museum," Gallagher remarked.

An entry in the guest book reinforces that impression: "I never knew there was such a great museum in New Jersey."

To counter the passive "museum look," the state park service provides visitors with hands-on experience. Recently 20 students from a public school in Jersey City helped Gallagher and his staff in the placement of nesting boxes in the salt marsh for barn owls, wood ducks and sparrow hawks.

There are bird walks, nature walks, beach walks, Arbor Day walks and canoeing along the waterfront between the park and Liberty and Ellis islands.

There are also programs on boating safety, trees, birds of prey and the salt marsh ecology.

In June, the interpretive center conducted a "Fish Tagging Day" with the American Littoral Society, a national marine organization based at Sandy Hook on the northern Jersey Shore. Participants tagged fish and released them at the Caven Point pier at the southerly edge of the park. The object of the exercise was to tag as many game species as possible as part of a study on Hudson River fisheries and habitats.

In the beach walks, waterfront wildlife is observed, including crabs and clams. Before the industrialization of the waterfront in the 19th Century, oysters were harvested from around the two Gateway islands.

The interpretive center has been set up to examine the relationship between human activity and the marine environment, as well as the various stages of development that took place over three centuries, from shipbuilding to manufacturing, transportation and, today, regulated recreation.

Preserved wildlife abounds inside the interpretive center, where owls, foxes, bald eagles, various species of fish and plant life are mounted for close-up scrutiny.

A diorama, or split box, depicts life on the water's edge, complete with lighthouse and sailboat on the horizon.

Educators who tour the center are given an introduction to the Gateway experience encompassing the Hudson River and harbor waterfronts. Prepared by the state Department of Environmental Protection, the literature reminds us that "our species' future existence depends upon a working knowledge of our environment ... a deep commitment to the continuing health of the planet."

Students are taught that the natural environment is "both a resource and liability—a resource that supplies us with food, water and shelter, a liability because the conservation and wise use of these resources are our responsibility."

To stimulate students into thinking about natural resources around them, the interpretive center is developing instructional programs for use in schools. For example, a multiplication exercise might simultaneously be a lesson in population dynamics, or a language arts exercise can also be a natural history lesson.

Class projects investigate such diverse interests as energy use, wetlands, forest/watershed management, hazardous substances, wildlife habitat management and environmental issues.

A program called "Save a Place" introduces the student to the "habitat" concept, in which the natural environment is studied for its ability to support various species of wildlife.

Programs at the interpretive center trace the uses of the area from the 15 Century when Indians flourished by fishing and hunting, to the advent of the steam engine and transportation and industrialization.

Specific sights in the guided tour are Jensen's Port at Communipaw, the Morris Canal and the landmark Central Railroad Terminal.

A 45-minute film titled "Dreams of Distant Shores" is available for classroom use. Produced by Public Service Electric & Gas Co., the documentary concentrates on the historical significance of the Statue of Liberty and the millions of immigrants she greeted as they entered the Gateway harbor.

Liberty State Park Development Corp.

To complete the improvements and other major projects in the 800-acre park, the state set up the Liberty State Park Development Corporation in 1984. Its mission is to balance the public and private demands made on this priceless Gateway real estate and to come up with the more than $200 million needed to make Liberty State Park the most popular, attractive, and dynamic urban waterfront recreational-educational experience in America in the 21st century.

The corporation's partnership with the state involves completion of the park's master plan approved in 1983. Among the major aspects of the plan are:

- *Liberty Walk*—a 1⅓ mile long, 35-foot wide, crescent-shaped promenade along the water's edge costing $34 million and doubling as a seawall. Because of the sweeping view of the harbor from Liberty Walk, it is the triumphant arc at America's Gateway.

- *Liberty Science Center and Hall of Technology* already in place featuring interactive exhibits.

- *Two marinas* for public use and a public boat launch ramp, along with open lawns for picnicking already in place.

- *A Park Lodge*—a small conference center with overnight guest accommodations.

- *An active recreation area*—a public pool complex and recreation facilities.

Liberty Science Center

The $50 million Science Center is oriented so that its major axis is in alignment with the Statue of Liberty and the new Omnitheater. This establishes a direct visual relationship between the Science Center, the Omnitheater, and the Statue of Liberty, giving visitors to the Tech Center framed distant views of Miss Liberty from within the building.

The 142,000-square-foot center is situated on a site to preserve adjacent existing wetlands, permitting outdoor nature exhibits to be augmented with natural science exhibits displayed within the center. Nature trails and wildlife observation areas within the wetlands are integrated into public educational programs on natural sciences.

Instead of extensive concrete retaining walls, or formal assemblages of masonry or stone construction often utilized in the design of bases for large buildings, an earth berm extends from three sides of the structure, serving as a landscaped transition zone between the human-designed environment at the center and the surrounding natural area of the park.

The tower is a recognizable landmark, prominently visible to tourists arriving at the park from Exit 14-B of the New Jersey Turnpike, or from across the harbor. The tower is also a symbol of the Science Center and a circular display area for exciting, kinetic exhibits. The porte cochere at the base of the tower heralds the entrance to the center and also functions as a covered entranceway for visitors arriving or leaving in vehicles.

The domed metal roof over the Omnitheater is a literal expression of the exterior of the science center; underneath, the unique domed shape serves as the projection screen for celestial showings or other cinematic presentations. The dome is an architecturally dominant termination to the rear of the center in juxtaposition to the tower at the front.

Exterior decks on the center are for extending spaces to the outdoors and providing settings more appropriate than interior spaces for the display of certain artifacts such as windmills and solar-powered equipment. Exterior decks accessible from the dining room attracts visitors to outdoor dining as seasons permit, providing an unobstructed view of the Gateway islands, Central Railroad Terminal, and the harbor.

Immediately upon entering the Science Center's main lobby, visitors arrive at one end of a four-story atrium space located in the center of the building. From this vantage point, they have the opportunity to experience an overview of the many activities and exhibits above and below them. From the atrium, visitors can travel from one exhibit space to another.

The second, or entrance floor, of the center functions as a "free zone" permitting visitors to gain access to the museum shop, a cafe, the Omnitheater, and the auditorium. The "free zone" serves as an extension of Liberty Park, giving visitors an opportunity to enter the building without paying an admission fee to view several exhibits, including the Omnimax Theater projection room, as well as to view some of the various exhibits beyond the "free zone" and to obtain a sense of wonderment about the activities and programs available for the public to enjoy.

Two spaces within the tower provide unique exhibits and activities in which visitors can participate. The observation room at the top of the tower enables visitors to observe spectacular views of the landscape and landmarks surrounding the Science Center. All areas of Liberty Park are clearly visible from this observation room.

Other public attractions open to the public in Liberty Park are described by signs within the tower room, enabling tourists to orient themselves relative to the Center and various points of interest in the park.

An opening at the center of the observation floor allows special exhibits to be suspended within the tower room which can be seen from above and below the observation room level. The tower room's height permits the display of many exhibits which would otherwise be too large for average exhibition gallery spaces.

Broad expanses of glass in the outer walls of the tower allows large illuminated exhibits to be seen from places remote from the Science Center. At nighttime, these are especially exciting when they are creatively illuminated and/or produce motions that can be seen from afar.

The architect is The Hillier Group in Princeton. The design architect is E. Verner Johnson and Associates of Boston.

Bibliography

"Liberty Park rises from rains," by Gordon Bishop, Star-Ledger Special Report, Second of a Series, *The Star-Ledger,* June 7, 1976.

"The gateway opens on Liberty ... " by Gordon Bishop, *The Star-Ledger,* June 15, 1976.

"Jersey launches Ellis ferry," by Gordon Bishop, *The Star-Ledger,* September 8, 1976.

The Central Railroad of New Jersey's First 100 years, 1849–1949, A Historical Survey, by Elaine Anderson, published by Center for Canal History and Technology; 1984.

"Sculptor chips out monument to Liberation," by Mark Finston, *The Star-Ledger*, February 23, 1985.

"World War II time capsule buries images of human nature's best and worst hours," by Mark Finston, *The Star-Ledger*, April 10, 1985.

"Monument to Freedom," by Lucy Schulte, *The Star-Ledger*, May 26, 1985.

"Memorial to Liberation" dedicated at Liberty Park, by Al Frank, *The Star-Ledger*, May 31, 1985.

"Melting pot experience takes form," by Gordon Bishop, *The Sunday Star-Ledger*, July 3, 1986.

Liberty Walk & Amphitheater, Waterfront Improvement Plan, Schematic Design Manual, State of New Jersey, November 1988.

Science Center, Summary Schematic Design Document, The Hillier Group, Princeton, for the New Jersey Department of Environmental Protection, March 27, 1989.

"The Historic Trilogy"—Statue of Liberty, Ellis Island, CRRNJ Terminal Building, New Jersey Division of Parks and Forestry, May 1989.

"Liberty Walk on Last Lap," by Al Frank, *The Sunday Star-Ledger*, October 29, 1989.

"Liberty State Park," by Al Frank, *The Sunday Star-Ledger*, November 12, 1989.

Chapter 5

Governors Island

Long before the Italian explorer Giovanni de Verrazano became probably the first European to see Governors Island when he sailed into the Upper New York Bay in 1524, the Leni Lenape natives called this wooded sanctuary "Pagganck," their name for the groves of nut trees covering the 175-acre island just off the tip of southern Manhattan. Later, the Dutch designation for the thick stands of oak, hickory, and chestnut trees in which the natives found shelter and food was "Nooten Eylandt," or "Nutten Island."

The formal or recorded history of the island, which served, until recently, as the largest Coast Guard base in the world, began on June 13, 1637, when the Dutch "bought" the isolated land from the Manhatas natives (for which Manhattan owes its geographic identity). Wouter Van Twiller, the Director General of New Netherlands, "purchased" Pagganck from two natives, Cakapeteyno and Pehiwas. The transaction involved two ax heads, a string of beads, and a few nails. Since the natives had no concept of ownership of land and natural resources, the "legal" transaction had no meaning to them. It was an abstract

GOVERNORS ISLAND
Building number 110, originally used as Army's barracks, became a search and rescue school for the Coast Guard. The school left in 1992. From then on the building was used as administrative offices.

piece of paper. The land was simply there for anyone who occupied it. And they were the original inhabitants of this land for thousands of years. Ownership and European legal documents had no meaning or validity in their culture, which spanned more than 10,000 years on the North American continent.

Not long after Van Twiller became Governor of the Dutch's new territory, he was charged with illegal trading—and incompetence. Realizing he was going to be replaced as Governor, Van Twiller decided to take Nutten Island for himself and arranged to receive the island as a personal grant. In 1638, Van Twiller was sent back to The Netherlands and his purchase of Nutten Island was declared in violation of the West India Company's Charter.

On July 1, 1652, the new Director General and Council formally annulled the purchase and returned Nutten Island to the public domain, the same status it enjoyed for thousands of years under the natives' presence. From then on, it was set aside as an estate for the Dutch governors and, later, for their English successors. Van Twiller was thus probably the only "private owner" of the island since it surfaced in the harbor after the last Ice Age some 12,000 years ago as a little sand bar.

In 1644, the English captured New Amsterdam and renamed it New York (after the Duke of York). They also took Nutten Island, which the Dutch had failed to fortify despite its strategic location at the point of Manhattan Island. In 1653, during the third Anglo-Dutch War, the Dutch regained their lost province, only to lose it again to England under the terms of the Treaty of Westminster in 1674.

In 1698, the island was set aside by the Assembly as being "part of the Denizen of His Majestie's Fort at New York for the benefit and accommodation of his Majestie's Governors for the time being." By an Act of Legislature on March 29, 1784, it was

GOVERNORS ISLAND
Bird's eye view (from a plane) of Governors Island. Lower Manhattan is on the left, downtown Brooklyn is on the right, and the famous Brooklyn Bridge is at the left center.

named "The Governor's Island." Gradually "The" and the apostrophe (') in "Governor's" was dropped, leaving the title as it is today—Governors Island. As federal property, it is owned by all American citizens.

From 1691 to 1702, the English Colonial Governors urged the fortification of New York Harbor. Their efforts, however, resulted in only 1,500 British Pounds committed to the defenses at "The Narrows" separating Staten Island from Brooklyn. The 1,500 Pounds was "appropriated" in 1702 by Lord Cornbury for the construction of a mansion on Governors Island, hardly considered even then as a "fortification." Lord Cornbury's island dwelling was also financed by a series of unique taxes, including a levy of 5 shillings and a sixpence on every bachelor over the age of 25.

The grand structure was erected on high ground on the northeast end of the island and was used by Lord Cornbury and, later, Governor. It was fittingly named "The Smiling Garden of the Sovereigns of the Province." It subsequently served as a guard house and headquarters of the island's garrison. Its cellar then contained the famous "Black Hole," a cell for the solitary confinement of difficult prisoners. The old "Governor's Mansion" also served as the Senior Officer's home until the Commanding General's Quarters were erected in 1840.

There is a legend that during the American Revolution the house was connected by a tunnel to a private dock on Buttermilk Channel by which the British Governor could escape to his official barge if the warring colonists landed on the island. Although there is no trace of the rumored tunnel today, it was supposed to have been large enough to accommodate the Governor's coach and four horses.

In 1710, the colonial authorities designated Governors Island a quarantine station for large groups of Palatines arriving in America from West Germany. Between 7,000 and 10,000 camped on the island at one time. One of those refugees was John Peter Zenger, who became publisher of the *New York Weekly Journal* and the first famous defender of the freedom of the press in the New World (the First Amendment in the Constitution). The Palatines came from Palatinate, a district in southwest Germany, west of the Rhine. It belonged to Bavaria until 1945. The Palatinate was a territory under the jurisdiction of a Palatine, someone having royal privileges.

During the 18th century, the island was used as a lumber mill, plantation, recreation area, and game preserve.

Troops were stationed on the island for the first time in 1755. The first garrison was the 51st Regiment of British Colonial Militia under the command of an American-born major-general, Sir William Pepperell. A native of Maine, Pepperell had been Commander-in-Chief of the New England force that captured the French fortress of Louisburg during the French-Indian War. The 51st Regiment was soon joined by the 22nd Regiment of Foot, the 44th Regiment of Foot, and the 62nd Regiment of Foot, called the "Royal Americans."

The 62nd Regiment was a locally recruited unit of the British Regular Army. It was organized at Governors Island in 1755 and remained there for many years. In 1757, the 62nd Regiment was renamed "The Royal American Regiment, H.M. 60th Regiment of Foot" and, as the King's "Royal Rifle Corps," is still an active unit of the British Army. Lord Jeffrey Amherst was one of the Regiment's early commanders, and Horatio Gates, later Adjutant General of the Continental Army, served as an officer in the Royal Americans. There were four battalions in the Regiment and one was known as the "Governors Island Battalion."

The Revolutionary War

The years before the American Revolution were quiet on the island. There was little activity and the defenses were neglected. Suddenly the "rebellious" New York was threatened by the British. American Revolutionary War General Israel Putnam and 1,000 troops arrived to aid Colonel Prescott's famous Bunker Hill (Boston) Regiment already stationed on the island. During the night of April 9, 1776, the troops labored to throw up defenses against the British fleet. By August, the island defenses had been built and were considered one of the strongest American posts.

GOVERNORS ISLAND
Winter landscape with Lower Manhattan in the background.
Cannon of Fort Jay (1798) in foreground guarding New York City.

On September 15, 1776, the British occupied New York, including the island. The War for Independence moved up the Hudson River. Governors Island, although garrisoned and fortified, remained inactive. In 1783, with peace and reoccupation by the Americans, Governors Island changed hands for the last time. The island returned to military control in 1794. With the threat of war with France, it was again garrisoned by the U.S. Army and remained under their control for the next 172 years.

In 1790, Alexander Hamilton, the first Secretary of the Treasury in the new Republic headed by President George Washington, formed the Revenue Cutter Service, the forerunner of the United States Coast Guard. The Coast Guard's motto is "Semper Paratus," or "Always Ready." The Coast Guard is at all times one of America's armed forces. In peacetime, it serves as an agency under the U.S. Department of Transportation (DOT). In wartime, it is part of the United States Navy.

During the War of 1812 with the British, Governors Island was a solidly fortified deterrent, protecting New York and its environs. It later served as a departure point for troops during the Mexican War and as a recruiting station during the Civil War.

Many of the structures put up in the 17th and 18th centuries are preserved as national historic landmarks. "The Governor's House" is the oldest building on the island. Built in 1708 as the residence for the British Governor of the New York colony, the Governor's House was the home, until recently, of the Commanding Office of the Coast Guard's "Support Center New York." The original structure was substantially altered in 1749 and has been modified many times since.

Construction of Fort Jay began in 1794 and was completed in 1798. It was named after the Secretary of Foreign Affairs, John Jay. The design of the fort—a star-shaped irregular pentagon—was inspired by the distinguished French architect Sebastien de Vauban, the military engineer to Louis XIV. The gateway to the fort is surmounted by a flamboyant sculptured trophy composed of flags, cannon, small weapons, banded faces with a liberty cap, and, dominating it all, a spread eagle. Once boasting a hundred guns, its massive walls appeared impenetrable. So intimidating to any passing ship, Fort Jay was never attacked, not even by the British in the War of 1812. The fort was rebuilt and renamed Fort Columbus in 1803. The change in name is believed to have been caused by the unpopularity of the Treaty with England, which Jay negotiated in 1795. The original name was restored in 1904. The Fort was used as a family housing unit until recently.

An Island of Many Houses

Castle Williams, completed in 1811 and alternately known as the "Tower" and "Cheesebox," is named in honor of Colonel Jonathan Williams, who at the time was Superintendent of West Point Military Academy and Chief Engineer of the U.S. Army. Its walls of Newark red sandstone are some 40 feet high and seven to eight feet thick. The castle was protected by 27 French 35-pounder cannons lining the

GOVERNORS ISLAND
*Castle Williams (1811) on the right has a "twin,"
Castle Clinton in Manhattan's Battery Park. Lower Manhattan is in the background.*

lower tier and 39 20-pounders on the second tier. Castle Williams and Castle Clinton in lower Manhattan's Battery Park were put up as twin forts to guard the channel between Governors Island and New York City. Castle Clinton once was used as an immigration depot before Ellis Island. Castle Williams was also used as a fort and then a prison by the Army from Civil War days until 1966.

The Admiral's House was built in 1840 and served as the Commanding General's Quarters until Governors Island was turned over to the Coast Guard in 1966. The house contains 27 rooms and, at one time, was the home of World War I General John J. Pershing, the first commander of the First Army. It was the home of the Coast Guard Atlantic Area commander until 1997.

The Blockhouse was built in the 1840s and has served as a blockhouse, headquarters, hospital, and officer's quarters. The

GOVERNORS ISLAND
Governors Island lighthouse.

Officers Club in the South Battery was erected in 1812. It was planned as a defense for Buttermilk Channel, the strip of water between the island and Brooklyn.

The Dutch House was built in 1845. It is an authentic copy of an early Dutch settler's home and was used as a storehouse until 1920.

In 1800, New York State ceded the island to the U.S. government. By 1912, the federal government had added more than 100 acres to the island.

Flights of Fancy

Aviation history was made on Governors Island on September 29, 1909 when Wilbur Wright made the first flight from the island around the Statue of Liberty. Another historic flight occurred the following year on May 29 when Glen Curtis landed on the island to complete his flight from Albany, New York, and win a $10,000 prize offered by Joseph Pulitzer, publisher of the *New York World*. During the next few years other flights from the island were made by aviation pioneers. From May 1916 to March 1917 an aviation training center was operated on the island. With approval of Major General Leonard Wood, commander of Governors Island, a group of civilians established the flying school to promote the development of military aviation. A memorial in honor of those early flights was erected on the south side of Liggett Hall on December 17, 1954 by the "Early Birds," an organization of "those who flew here before 1916."

In recognition of shared traditions, the officers and men of the King's Royal Rifle Corps presented their only ancient Royal American Regimental Color to Governors Island on January 9, 1921. The inscription accompanying the gift read, in part, "to serve as a memento that the Royal American Regiment and the Regiments of New York fought shoulder to shoulder, not only during the many years of warfare which ended in the conquest of New France and the subjugation of the Indian tribes bordering on the Great Lakes, but also, after a century and a half, against a common enemy in a more terrible European conquest."

This regimental flag now hangs on the north wall of the Chapel of Saint Cornelius the Centurion, the Protestant chapel built in 1905 by the Trinity Parish of New York.

The Coast Guard

During a June 30, 1966 joint ceremony, the United States Army ended its 172-year stay on Governors Island. Rear Admiral I. J. Stephens accepted the island for the Coast Guard, as a battery of guns saluted his flag flying over Fort Jay.

Coast Guard Support Center (formerly Coast Guard Base, New York) was established to operate Governors Island and its facilities. The staffs housed on the island are those of the Commander, Atlantic Area; the Commander of the Atlantic Maritime Defense Zone; and the Commander of the Atlantic Maintenance and Logistics Command.

Also on the island were the Captain of the Port and Commander, Group New York; the New York Coast Guard Training Center; and the New York Vessel Traffic System and Station.

The island also served as the homeport for Coast Guard Cutters Dallas, Gallatin, Penobscot Bay, Sorrell, Red Beech, Wire, Hawser Line, and Sturgeon Bay.

Governors Island was home, until its closing in 1997, to more than 4,000 member-residents of the Coast Guard and their families, as well as 1,700 civilian and military members who commute to the island daily to work. Linked to the southern tip of Manhattan by a short ferry ride, the island was a self-contained community and is listed as a National Historic Site. On this island community were medical and dental care services, commissaries, exchanges, barber shops, beauty parlors, country stores, delicatessens, cafeterias, a bowling center, Officers, CPO and Enlisted Clubs, package stores, security, the *Governors Island Gazette* (the weekly island newspaper), and even a Burger King.

Members of the three chapels—Catholic, Jewish, and Protestant—worked together in ecumenical harmony. The faculties of the Child Development Center and Billard

108 Gateway to America

GOVERNORS ISLAND
Support Center, Police, Post Office at Governors Island.

Elementary School (Public School 26) worked closely with the numerous resident volunteers to ensure the island's children receive the best possible education.

The Coast Guard's Special Services Division maintained athletic and recreation facilities, including an arts and crafts shop, handball and racquetball courts, auto craft shop, playgrounds, tennis courts, gymnasium, movie theater, nine-hole golf course, softball fields, community center, library, swimming pools, and picnic grounds.

There are more than 225 buildings on Governors Island, of which 38 were constructed prior to 1900 and 12 since the Coast Guard took over the island in 1966.

The Coast Guard is known for its search and rescue duties, coastal defense, military readiness, drug interdiction responsibilities, and providing aircraft and ships to assist any vessel or individual in distress on the water.

The Coast Guard also has a variety of other responsibilities: pollution prevention and control, port security, merchant marine safety, aids to navigation, boating safety, polar and domestic ice-breaking, oceanographic and weather observation services, and the enforcement of federal laws on the U.S. waters.

The men and women of the Coast Guard protect life and property at sea—and the sea itself. The Coast Guard has approximately 38,000 officers and enlisted personnel and nearly 5,000 civilian employees.

In recent years, Governors Island has been the site for many historical events. On July 4, 1986, President Ronald Reagan and French President François Mitterand relit the torch of the Statue of Liberty for its centennial celebration, known on the island as "Op-Sail 1986" (the first Operation Sail was for the nation's bicentennial in 1976). The torch was illuminated when President Reagan touched a button (for a laser beam) on a ceremonial platform in Liberty Village, a residential area of Governors Island.

In the spring of 1988, delegates from the United States, South Africa, Cuba, and Angola met on the island to negotiate

GOVERNORS ISLAND
Ferry ready to leave for Manhattan in the background.

peace talks in a 13-year-old guerrilla war in southern Africa. Their meeting established a peace treaty that is still in effect.

In December 1988, President Reagan and his vice president, George Bush, met for a historic luncheon meeting with the Soviet Union's General Secretary, Mikhail Gorbachev. Though the meeting was not considered a "Summit," it was an important stepping stone ultimately leading to the dissolution of the Soviet Union and a return to independent democratic Republics.

Governors Island—A National Monument

In January 2001, Governors Island was declared a "national monument" by the federal government. The two historic forts and their surrounding areas on 22 acres of the island's 161 acres are now preserved as national treasures. The remaining acreage is being divided among three uses: education, culture, and recreation.

The City University of New York (CUNY) will establish a satellite campus on Governors Island. New York City's various museums will establish extensions on the harbor island, and New York City will create a public park for visitors and tourists to enjoy at the entranceway to the Gateway of America.

Governors Island will remain a highly visible place for the public to enjoy.

Directions

Governors Island can be reached by ferry from lower Manhattan.

Bibliography

Overview of Governors Island, Howard J. Holmes, Public Affairs, U.S. Coast Guard, 1989.

"Welcome to Governors Island—A Historic Military Island," official pamphlet of the U.S. Coast Guard, 1989.

"History of Governors Island," a fact sheet compiled by the U.S. Coast Guard.

"Self-Guided Walking Tour of Historic Governors Island," provided by the U.S. Coast Guard.

"History Preserved—A Guide to New York City Landmarks and Historic Districts," by Harmon H. Goldstone and Martha Dalrymple, Simon & Schuster; New York, 1974.

The World Book Encyclopedia, Volume 18, 1987.

Chapter 6

World Trade Center Memorial Chapter

At one time they soared as the world's tallest twin towers, the center of America's trading activities taking in the most spectacular view of the Gateway from the highest outdoor viewing platform on the planet—the rooftop promenade protruding into the morning misty clouds at a dizzying 1,377 feet.

The observation deck above the 110th floor of Two World Trade Center attracted more than 1.5 million visitors a year. On a clear day one could literally see to the distant horizons ... from the shores of Long Island and New Jersey, out over the Atlantic Ocean, up the Hudson River, and all the way to the Appalachian mountains of Pennsylvania. Viewers who could stand such lofty sights could also browse in a gift shop along the promenade or refresh themselves at a quick-service restaurant. The deck was open seven days a week from 9:30 A.M. to 9:30 P.M.

An enclosed deck on the 107th floor featured a "History of Trade" exhibit.

The towers' "Skylobby" elevator systems separated express from local runs. There were 99 elevators, including 33 express elevators, in each tower. Each express elevator could handle 55 people for a total capacity of 100,000 pounds.

A 360-foot television mast extending above One World Trade Center was completed in May 1979. The giant needle supported 10 main television antennas, numerous auxiliary antennas, and a master FM antenna. The metro region's television stations and two UHF stations broadcasted from the mast.

An exquisite dining room and bar at One World Trade Center, appropriately called the "Windows of the World," provided another panoramic view from the 107th floor. A ballroom on the 106th floor accommodated up to 1,000 guests.

There were, in all, 22 dining areas in the world trade complex offering a sumptuous range of restaurants and food services, including banquet and meeting rooms.

More than 60 shops, restaurants, and services were located on the World Trade Center Concourse, on the 44th-floor "Skylobby" of One World Trade Center, and the Observation Deck. The shops ranged in size from a large department store to small specialty boutiques.

Each floor of the twin towers covered one square acre. The 220 acres of rental space in the twin towers were enclosed by 43,600 windows. The more than 600,000 square feet of glass were cleaned by automatic window-washing machines that traveled on stainless steel tracks.

Some 60,000 people worked in the World Trade Center, with another 100,000 business and leisure visitors coming to the center daily.

Sometimes dubbed the "King Kong Towers" (from the scene of the 1970s remake of the great ape film classic), the World Trade Center was actually a series of high-rises dominated by the imposing, square towers. The world trade complex consisted of the landmark blockish towers, a 47-story building identified as Seven World Trade Center, two nine-story office buildings at Four and Five World Trade Center, an eight-story U.S. Customhouse at Six World Trade Center (the most modern in the U.S.), and a 22-story hotel at Three World Trade Center known as Vista International New York. Together, they represented approximately 12 million square feet of rental space.

World Trade Center Memorial Chapter 115

WORLD TRADE CENTER
The Twin Towers seen from the Hudson River.

The buildings were all constructed around a central five-acre landscaped Plaza. All seven buildings had entrances to the Plaza, as well as to the surrounding city streets around Manhattan's Wall Street business district.

Vista International New York was the first major hotel built in lower Manhattan since 1836. The 825-room luxury hotel, initially operated by Hilton International and then Marriott, was replete with first-class, full-meeting facility amenities for business and leisure travelers for conventions, meetings, and receptions.

The Trade Center's Concourse, located immediately below the five-acre Plaza, was the largest enclosed shopping mall in Manhattan. It served as the main interior pedestrian circulation level for the entire complex.

Prominent pieces of modern art and sculpture embellished the Plaza, the tower mezzanines, and surrounding walks. They included works by Alexander Calder, Louise Nevelson, Joan Miro, Fritz Koenig, James Rosati, and Masaynki Nagare.

WORLD TRADE CENTER
International Plaza at the World Trade Center. Bronze Sphere for Plaza Fountain by German sculptor Fritz Koenig, installed in 1972. The remains of this sculpture were saved for public viewing after September 11, 2001. The sculpture is permanently installed in Battery Park as a memorial.

WORLD TRADE CENTER
Memorial Fountain for the victims of the World Trade Center bombing on February 26, 1993. A bomb set by terrorists exploded below this site.

The twin towers, each rising 1,350 feet, were the tallest buildings in New York City and the third tallest in the world (the largest are the twin Petronas Towers in Kuala Lumpur City Center in Malaysia, completed in 1997; the second tallest is the Sears Tower in Chicago, which opened in 1973). Each floor was approximately one acre in size. The floors were column-free, assuring maximum flexibility in layout.

Conceived in January 1960

How did this unprecedented architectural/construction project come about? In January 1960, the Downtown Lower Manhattan Association recommended development of a World Trade Center by the Port Authority of New York and New Jersey, the world's largest public authority. In March 1961, the Port Authority issued a report recommending establishment of a World Trade Center. The two states envisioned it as the headquarters for international trade within the bistate port district encompassing the largest and most diversified metropolitan region in America, consisting of the five boroughs of New York City; the four suburban New York counties of Nassau, Rockland, Suffolk, and Westchester; and the eight counties of northern New Jersey—Bergen, Essex, Hudson, Middlesex, Morris, Passaic, Somerset, and Union. (The Port Authority was established on April 30, 1921, the first interstate agency created under the Constitution permitting compacts between states with Congressional consent. The Port District embraces a 25- mile radius of the Statue of Liberty.)

In February–March of 1962, legislation was enacted by the states of New York and New Jersey authorizing development of the World Trade Center and "related acquisition by the Port Authority of the Hudson and Manhattan Railroad"—now the Port Authority Trans-Hudson (PATH) system, a rail transit line linking the two states sharing the Hudson River.

In January 1964, architectural plans were unveiled by Minoru Yamasaki and Associates of Troy, Michigan, and Emery Roth and Sons of New York, designers of the World Trade Center.

The 16-acre site selected by the Port Authority stretched from Church Street on the east to West Street on the west, and from Liberty Street on the south to Barclay and Vesey Streets on the north.

The total Port Authority investment in the complex reached more than $1.2 billion when completed in the 1990s.

Excavation of the twin towers site began in August 1966, with the first steel girders going into place in August 1968. More than 1.2 million cubic yards of earth and rock were removed to make way for the Trade Center. The excavated material was placed nearby in the Hudson River, creating 23.5 acres of new land deeded to the City of New York. That landfill is now occupied by Battery Park City, itself a mini-city rivaling Rockefeller Center.

More than 200,000 tons of steel, far more than the amount required for the construction of the Verrazano-Narrows Bridge, went into the erection of the twin towers. The 425,000 cubic yards of concrete used in the towers were enough to build

World Trade Center Memorial Chapter 119

WORLD TRADE CENTER LOBBY
Seventy-five-foot high lobby mezzanine space of the North Tower
(One World Trade Center), June 2001.

WORLD TRADE CENTER
Tuesday, September 11, 2001.

World Trade Center Memorial Chapter 121

WORLD TRADE CENTER
Remains of the North Tower (One World Trade Center).

WORLD TRADE CENTER
Eleven-year-old Violetta Koss.
Photo taken on September 14, 2001, from the Newport waterfront.

a five-foot wide sidewalk from New York City to Washington, D.C. At peak periods of construction, some 3,500 workers were on the site daily.

In December 1970, the first tenant moved into One World Trade Center (the North Tower). In January 1972, the first tenant moved into Two World Trade Center (the South Tower).

The World Trade Center was dedicated on April 4, 1973 by New York Governor Nelson Rockefeller and New Jersey Governor William Cahill, both Republicans.

The U.S. Customs Service moved into Six World Trade Center in January 1974. The World Trade Center Observation Deck opened in December 1975. The Windows of the World restaurant opened in April 1976. The first tenant moved into Four World Trade Center in January 1977, and the Vista International New York Hotel officially opened at Three World Trade Center in July 1981.

The World Trade Center brought under one roof the full spectrum of businesses and governmental agencies involved in marketing, financing, processing, insuring, documenting, and transporting international trade. The more than 1,200 firms and organizations were engaged in almost every conceivable kind of international commerce activity, including import, export, freight forwarding, customhouse brokerage, international banking and finance, insurance, transportation, trade associations, and foreign government representation.

The Trade Center was also the Manhattan headquarters for the Port Authority's administrative staff and for agencies of the State of New York.

Four World Trade Center was New York's headquarters for commodities trading. The Commodity Exchange; the New York Coffee, Sugar, and Cocoa Exchange; the New York Cotton Exchange; and the New York Mercantile Exchange all shared a joint trading floor for commodities, and gold and other precious metals.

World Trade Institute

The World Trade Institute, operated by the Port Authority, was located on the 55th floor of One World Trade Center. The Institute was the World Trade Center's school for international business and finance. Conferences, seminars, and courses in numerous aspects of foreign trade were offered for all levels of management. The Institute's Language School provided specialized instruction in 15 different languages and dialects. More than 600 seminars, courses, and international training programs were offered by the Institute in any given year. More than 60 courses were offered by the Evening School of World Trade, as well as 400 Language School classes. Twelve international training programs have been conducted in one year for the benefit of participants from developing countries.

The Port Authority also developed a business simulation game called "Export to Win" that can be played on a personal computer. It is designed to help staff of small and medium-sized companies improve their understanding of the export process and determine their exporting potential. Produced under a grant from the U.S. Economic Development Administration, the program simulates dynamic market conditions.

More than 100 Chinese port officials have participated in a port management training program in China organized by the World Trade Institute. Sponsored by the China Science and Technologies Exchange Center, the program was an outgrowth of a 1987 Port Authority trade mission to the People's Republic of China.

The World Trade Center was easily accessible by mass transit. Stations of the three major New York City subway systems—the IRT, BMT, and IND—were located within the Center. Air-conditioned PATH trains also sped interstate commuters between the Trade Center and four New Jersey communities: Hoboken, Jersey City, Harrison, and Newark. Below-grade parking accommodated almost 2,000 cars. Parking was free with proof of a $10 purchase in any Concourse store or restaurant.

World Trade Center Memorial Chapter 125

WORLD TRADE CENTER TRIBUTE IN LIGHT
Monday, March 11, 2002.

September 11, 2001

The World Trade Center twin towers were destroyed by a terrorist attack on September 11, 2001 just before and after 9 A.M. The future of the prominent World Trade Center site will be a lasting tribute to the 2,801 police officers, fire fighters, and twin towers workers who perished in the worst terrorist attack in history. As this book goes to print, there are many creative and diverse plans to build an American classical trade center around "ground zero," where the original World Trade Center disintegrated in a towering inferno. A fitting memorial will be erected at ground zero itself, where the two soaring towers once stood as a symbol of America's free enterprise system, the greatest the world has ever known.

From the ashes of the fallen towers will rise a monument to the victims of the "9/11" disaster. The new World Trade Center monument will reflect the spirit of freedom and liberty, the cornerstones of America's enduring Constitutional Republic.

The victims will never be forgotten.

Bibliography

FACT SHEET: The World Trade Center in the Port of New York-New Jersey, prepared by the Port Authority May 1989, One World Trade Center; New York, NY 10048.

Comprehensive Annual Financial Report for the year ended December 31, 1988. Prepared by the Port Authority of NY & NJ.

Chapter 7

Battery Park City

It stands out in the lower Hudson River like the prized jewel in the crown. As the sparkling eye of the Hudson River waterfront looking out over the Gateway to America, Battery Park City is the newest and most elegant urban setting in the United States, a unique "mini-city" built atop a 92-acre landfill in the Hudson River in front of the World Trade Center site. When filled to capacity, Battery Park City is the home for a modern new community of 25,000 residents, plus 50,000 workers.

Without the World Trade Center, however, there could not have been a Battery Park City, for this waterfront gem owes its unique existence to the excavated earthen materials from the twin towers.

It was a bold experiment in urban design and planning, from its daring conception as a public/private partnership between New York City and State and the entrepreneurial venture capital needed to create a magnificent community on a barren landfill of rock and sand sticking out into a historic tributary. Although much of Manhattan Island was built on fill pushing the water's edge ever farther into the Hudson and East Rivers and Upper New York Bay, the landfill that gave birth to Battery Park City was an imaginative and, ultimately, successful challenge in creating an instant urban-marine environment blending the best of the old with the exploratory and surprising new without making it look like a peninsular appendage to the "Big Apple."

What could have been a $4 billion architectural/construction fiasco became, instead, the enviable model of urban planning for the 21st century. All new waterfront developments should radiate such beauty and balance in form and function!

Integrated into the sensitively structured densities of commercial and residential buildings of complementary shapes and sizes is a pleasant, intricate network of plazas and gardens, parks and coves, esplanades, pathways and public squares, and commons. In all, they comprise one-third, or about 30 acres, of precious open space in this waterfront city-within-a-city.

New York Times architectural critic Paul Goldberger calls it "close to a miracle," citing its "sense of place" and comparing it to Rockefeller Center as "one of the better pieces of urban design of modern times."

The architecture ranges from "decent to impressive," Goldberger observed, which for New York in the 1980s was "practically perfection."

The dazzling centerpiece of Battery Park City is the World Financial Center, a collection of five mammoth office towers handsomely shaped with setbacks culminating in "geometrically shaped tops—a pyramid tops one tower, a low dome another." The *Times* reviewer found the varied tops and different heights differentiate the towers, and that identical facades tie them together. In a reflection of modern romanticism, the buildings are sheathed in a mix of granite and glass, with more granite on the lower levels and more glass above, so that the towers seem both lighter and more modern as they rise.

The almost fantasylandlike story of Battery Park City is rooted in historic New York. The southern tip of Manhattan is the birthplace of New York City, where George Washington was sworn in as the first President of the United States. The seaport along the lower Hudson River and Bay bustled with commerce. The Stock Exchange was founded there. Fashionable neighborhoods emerged around this hub of thriving business and commerce. For nearly three centuries, life prospered for those who chose to live and work where Manhattan Island met the New York Bay.

By the 1960s, however, business was shifting to mid-Manhattan and New York City's first center of activity was slowly declining due to rising taxes and labor costs.

New York Governor Nelson Rockefeller envisioned a new New York City anchored by the world's tallest skyscrapers and an exciting mini-city built on the 25 acres of rubble removed from the huge foundations dug deep to bedrock for the twin towers. When the towers were erected, they were the tallest man-made structures on Earth (succeeded only by Chicago's Sears Tower a few years later).

Battery Park City Authority

To manage the development of this new city-within-a-city, the New York State Legislature created the Battery Park City Authority in 1968. The Authority is a public benefit corporation charged with constructing and developing the landfill site west of the World Trade Center site.

At first, conceptual plans called for a futuristic city organized in "PODS" of clustered housing, with a commercial area at the southern end of the landfill and two separate levels for pedestrian and vehicular circulation. But the New York City fiscal crisis of the mid-1970s fortuitously vanquished this voguish and separate appendage to Manhattan Island.

By 1979, a Master Plan was designed by Alexander Cooper and Stanton Eckstut to make Battery Park City a distinct and vital part of New York City. Private investors were impressed with the details and scope of the plan. By extending the existing street grid into Battery Park City, and by preserving clear views to the Hudson River, the new plan emphatically underscored the importance of keeping the city-within-a-city concept intact.

BATTERY PARK CITY
Public promenade along the Hudson River offers a spectacular view.
In the background upper right, tops of the World Trade Center towers.

The investors "bought in"—and New York responded with a dramatic and workable plan to benefit all participants.

The Master Plan placed the World Financial Center in the heart of the development, connected it to the World Trade Center with two pedestrian bridges, and provided access to the Trade Center's above- and below-ground transportation facilities. A continuous 1.2 mile-long riverfront Esplanade linked the commercial center and its enormous public plaza with the new residential neighborhoods north and south of the World Financial Center.

The design guidelines for Battery Park City were scrupulously detailed requirements that went far beyond the most progressive zoning regulations anywhere. They assured the highest architectural and planning standards by restricting the size, shape, placement, and even the facade materials of each building. All structures had to have stone bases and masonry surfaces, prominent cornice lines to visually link the new buildings to typical older ones nearby, and varied rooflines to complement the spires of the Wall Street financial district. The design emphasis was always on the human scale: Variety was purposely pursued to provide both complexity and interest. The resulting architecture interpreted, rather than mimicked, New York City's most durable successes.

As the hub of Battery Park City, the World Financial Center's five towers with geometric copper roofs offered a distinctive new skyline and provided a visual counterpoint to the World Trade Center just across West Street. Developed by Olympia & York and designed by renowned architect Cesar Pelli, the World Financial Center is the new home to some of Wall Street's most prestigious firms—Merrill Lynch, American Express, Dow Jones, and Oppenheimer.

The main attraction of the World Financial Center is the Winter Garden, a glass-and-marble agora that has become New York City's most appealing venue for music, dance, and other live performing arts. In its first year, the Winter Garden and its adjacent riverside plaza hosted a variety of visual arts displays and some 50 free afternoon and evening performances running the stylistic gamut from the Vienna Boys' Choir and the Herbie Hancock Trio to a troupe of Siberian dancers and the Basel Ballet. In one concert billed as "Meet the Moderns," jazz, rock, and orchestral music were presented by a 30-piece chamber orchestra of the Brooklyn Philharmonic.

The Winter Garden, part of a seven-acre network of public spaces within the Financial Center, is a multifaceted attraction combining an arts center with a grand public space—the architectural nexus of an eight-million-square-foot office complex. A fan-shaped staircase descends into a spacious indoor piazza fashioned from granite and four types of Italian marble. Beyond a symmetrical grove of 16 palm trees reaching heights of 40 feet, the Garden's steel-girded glass portals overlook the Hudson River, and above its 120-foot high vaulted glass ceiling loom the American Express and Merrill Lynch towers. Set at the foot of each palm tree are new light-green metal benches whose gentle curves nicely echo the form of the huge, horseshoe-shaped atrium.

The Plaza is a 3.5-acre park surrounding the North Cove with a variety of spaces for public gatherings, strolling, and dining. The Plaza was designed for many everyday needs: the tourist making a one-time visit, the office worker eating lunch there regularly, the resident of lower Manhattan out for a stroll or run, and the frequent or occasional visitor from other parts of the city simply seeking a refreshing change of pace for a few hours.

The Plaza

The park setting is a coordinated series of eight unified but distinct spaces. The range of open spaces was designed to accommodate the individual, small intimate groups, and larger public gatherings. The Plaza can handle the enormous flow of people from the office buildings, their interior courtyards and colonnades, as well as the north and south arms of the Battery Park City Esplanade—and even some water traffic from the river itself!

The Plaza is a major intersection for all of the different patterns of pedestrian traffic. Dining areas are separated from the

BATTERY PARK CITY
Public sculpture.

more public areas by shallow linear reflecting pools, or flumes. Water spilling over the outer edges of the pools catches the light and creates a background of gentle sound. Below the pools, two tiers of steps descend to a row of stone tables and chairs providing informal eating facilities corresponding to the outdoor restaurant dining on the upper level. The tiered steps also serve as outdoor furniture for informal, amphitheaterlike gathering places. The steps are interrupted irregularly by a series of projections which, with the addition of curved railings, form seating groups for people-watching or contemplating the harbor views.

South of the Plaza's Terrace and planned in contrast to it is the Court. Dominated by a shallow sunken trapezoidal area paved with cobble and grass and bordered by a granite wall, this defined space was designed to accommodate changing exhibits of outdoor sculpture or small architectural structures. Its continuous border of three granite steps provides seating when the central space is used for public festivities or performances.

The Plaza's Summer Park along the Liberty Street ramp to the Esplanade is divided into a pair of landscaped zones. One zone, symmetrically planted with a grove of trees in a granite-paved surface, acts as a buffer to the traffic. It provides a more formal, urban park environment in contrast to the second zone bordering on the Esplanade, where a more informal, rustic style of planting provides a shaded retreat for the summer months.

The West Park is a counterpart to the Summer Park. Since this area receives the most direct sunlight for the longest period of the day, its layout encourages use in the early spring and late fall when the warmer thermal environment is desirable. The West Park resembles the rustic zone of the Summer Park, but with the addition of rough-hewn boulders as furniture for basking.

The Arc

The focal point of the entire Plaza is the Arc, a segment of a circle that projects over the water along the inland edge of the North Cove. Conceived as a balcony over the water, the Arc is located at the geometric center of the Plaza's waterside edge, where it forms a visually climactic destination for both the Plaza visitor and the Esplanade stroller. Tying together the north and south arms of the Esplanade, the Arc unifies the Plaza's distinct spatial elements and links the Plaza to the water with a ramp, allowing visitors access to an observation point just above the river's surface.

The Battery Park City Plaza pioneers new professional roles and directions, notably toward collaboration. Rather than being brought in subsequent to the planning stages to create autonomous objects, or to act as consultants on aesthetic details, here the artists have collaborated with architect and landscape architect on all aspects of the design process.

New York Post real estate columnist Carter B. Horsley describes the Battery Park City experience as the "thrill of romance with diversity, immensity, and people." After a summer day's excursion, Horsley wrote: "On such days, the delineation of sharp edges and liveliness of reflective surfaces etch indelible images of the power of modern times and beat a festive

BATTERY PARK CITY
Battery Park City on the Hudson River waterfront with New York Bay beyond.

BATTERY PARK CITY
Public promenade on the Hudson River waterfront with luxury apartment buildings that enjoy magnificent views of New York Bay including Liberty Island and Ellis Island.

parade rhythm of great contrasts between soft rivers lapping against arching, chiseled cliffs."

Horsley believes that, through Battery Park City "New York can regain its stature as a mecca of urbane wonder."

The World Financial Center's "Main Street" is the Winter Garden, lined with a splendiferous mix of fine shops. The town square (the Courtyard) is alive with restaurants and cafés that spill out into the town green (the Plaza), perched on the edge of the Hudson.

This cosmopolitan Main Street offers something for everyone: a bakery café ... complete vision care and eyewear ... chocolates and chocolate novelties ... imported men's leather shoes, apparel, and accessories ... natural leather bags, attachés, and accessories ... sport and comfort shoes ... fashion hosiery ... leather business and fashion accessories ... gift ensembles ... food and drink from 10 A.M. to 10 P.M. seven days a week ... fine women's apparel and accessories ... compact disc store ... fine dining ... regional specialties and banquet facilities at the Hudson River ... high design home, office, and travel accessories ... elegant Chinese dining ... an American bistro and carry-out food ... a tropical bar, desserts, and fun food ... apparel and goods for land and sea ... leather briefcases, handbags, accessories, and luggage ... a colorful array of cards, invitations, and gift packaging ... total shoe care and shoeshine ... free office pickup and delivery ... original historical documents as works of art ... a salon and cosmetic department store for women and men ... for innovative floral design and special event planning, there is Twigs ... books, music recordings, magazines, and newspapers from around the world ... fresh and grilled foods from sunny climes ... and a travel office for those who visit this mini-Gotham.

While shopping and dining embellish the commercial center, open space serves the same purpose for Rector Place, a neighborhood designed for that special outdoor experience on the waterfront. Rector Park is the focal center of the nine-acre Rector Place neighborhood located on four blocks south of Gateway Plaza and the World Financial Center. The residential community surrounds Rector Park. The 2,210 rental and cooperative/condominium apartments spread out among 12 different

BATTERY PARK CITY
Lower Manhattan as seen across the Hudson River from Newport City Marina.

buildings, including townhouses, mid-sized structures, and high rises. The housing complexes have such names as Hudson River Towers, River Rose, Liberty House, Liberty Terrace, Liberty Court, Battery Pointe, The Soundings, and Park Place.

Rector Park

Rector Park is the focal open space and commons for Rector Place. It is approximately one acre and was designed as two separate parks which work together as a whole to provide a *residential address* for the neighborhood. In contrast to the Esplanade and other Battery Park City open spaces, Rector Park is inward-looking and contemplative in character. It was conceived in the tradition of Manhattan's Gramercy Park, providing an Old World elegance and charm to the neighborhood. Equal importance has been given to the residents' view from above and to the pedestrians at ground level.

The "eastern" park has a large, slightly raised oval lawn at its center, which is bordered by Caledonia granite curbing. Several trees, including dogwood, cherry, ginko, and honey locust, are arranged in the lawn in an informal manner. Woodmold bricks set on end in a herring-bone pattern encircle the lawn. Granite seating walls with 1939 World's Fair-style benches define the outside perimeter of the brick walkway. Additional benches are in a larger seating area under the shade of two yellow-wood trees.

The eastern and western borders of the "east" park are enclosed by traditional, six-foot high, wrought-iron railing pickets with cast iron spears, terminating in four granite piers. Flowering and evergreen shrubs, as well as flowering crabapples and 10 large American Holly trees, are between the iron railing fence and the seating areas. A 40-foot planter provides colorful seasonal displays of perennial and annual flowers. A traditional bluestone sidewalk set in a random pattern surrounds the entire eastern park.

The western park is dominated by a large rectangular raised lawn. The lawn is bordered by a granite curbing. Pear trees mark the four corners of the lawn. The park contains two garden "parterres" on the eastern and western ends, with flowering crabapples in the center of each. Two horseshoe-shaped walkways made of woodmold brick set on end in a herringbone pattern surround the two "parterres" and provide seating around their perimeters. Random cut bluestone surrounds the entire western park and also provides walkways within it.

The northern and southern sides of the park are open and provide seating on both sides under the shade of honey locust trees.

Entrances to Rector Park are from the east via double balustrade of carved pink granite which is ramped for easy access for the physically challenged. The balustrade is flanked by granite steps. From the west, the park is accessible from the waterfront Esplanade via a ramped granite entryway bordered by large granite planters with riverbirch and ferns.

Lighting of the park is from decorative poles topped with stylish Bishops Crook fixtures.

Bibliography

Battery Park City Fact Sheet, prepared by Battery Park City Authority Battery Park City Master Plan, design statement by Cooper, Eckstut Associates.

Plaza At Battery Park City's World Financial Center, a collaborative design by Siah Armagani and Scott Burton, artists; Cesar Pelli, architect, and M. Paul Friedberg, landscape architects. Battery Park City color brochure. Shop & Dine, The World Financial Center.

Rector Place Fact Sheet, Battery Park City Authority Rector Park Fact Sheet, Battery Park City Authority.

"Battery Park City Is a Triumph of Urban Design," *Architecture View*, Paul Goldberger; *The New York Times*, August 31, 1986.

"Brave New World," by Carter B. Horsley, REAL ESTATE, *The New York Post*, July 6,1989.

"A New State for High Art and High Finance," by Andrew L. Yarrow, *The New York Times*, May 19, 1989.

Chapter 8

South Street Seaport

Nautical history comes alive at South Street Seaport, where a nostalgic kaleidoscope of vintage vessels, galleries, boutiques, and shops takes visitors back to the romantic sailing era of the 19th century when South Street, just beyond and below the Brooklyn Bridge, was called the "Street of Ships."

Visitors can board historic ships that ply the waters of the East and Hudson Rivers and New York Harbor, taking in the memorable sights of the Statue of Liberty and Ellis Island.

Tourists can stroll through the Marketplace, or stand on the balcony of Pier 17 and view the tugs and tankers passing under the legendary Brooklyn Bridge.

Or, they can watch street performers near the Fulton Market Building and enjoy special concerts on the piers and holiday fireworks.

Vessels of every description lined these East River piers when America was coming of age. Seamen, immigrants, merchants and tradesmen crowded the cobblestone streets and the imposing marine buildings. This was the center of an emerging port city: the countinghouses and ship chandleries, the sail lofts,

SOUTH STREET SEAPORT
Tall ships are a major attraction at this historic waterfront.

SOUTH STREET SEAPORT
General view with Lower Manhattan in the background.

printing shops, sailors' bars, and flophouses that animated the extraordinary contribution of maritime enterprise to the growth of American commerce and culture.

At the Seaport's peak in the mid-19th century, this district was populated by wharf rats and con men, sailors and cartmen, beggars and aristocrats, all churning through roads of mud.

Tours of the working life in the old port begin daily at 2 and 4 P.M. at the Pier 16 ticketbooth. Follow the story of the people who lived and worked in America's greatest port. The 50-minute walk ends with a demonstration at Bowne & Co., Stationers.

The Fulton Fish Market tour begins on the first and third Thursdays at 6 and 7:45 A.M. from spring through fall. Take a behind-the-scenes walk through the largest wholesale fish market in the country and you'll learn firsthand about fishmongers, fish, folklore, and market tips.

Seaport Museum

The centerpiece of this famous seafaring district is the South Street Seaport Museum, celebrating old New York, the port city that rose to world preeminence in the 19th century. Museum sites include:

- **Titanic Memorial Lighthouse**—a unique memorial to those lost in the Titanic disaster of 1912.

- **Waterfront Photographer**—changing exhibits of contemporary and historic photographs.

- **Book & Chart Store**—books, navigational charts, posters—a haven for maritime and New York history buffs.

- **Curiosity Shop**—small treasures, nautical gifts, and jewelry.

SOUTH STREET SEAPORT
South Street Seaport museum.

- **Bowne & Co., Stationers**—try pulling the "Devil's tail" at a 19th century printing shop.

- **Museum Gallery**—changing exhibits illustrating New York's growth from a fur-trading post to a bustling metropolis.

- **Melville Library**—a special research center, by appointment only.

- **Small Craft Collection**—traditional wooden boats displayed in the Ocean Reef Grille atop the Fulton Market Building.

- **Children's Center**—exhibits, hands-on workshops, holiday and maritime programs.

- **Norway Galleries**—once a China trader's countinghouse, now a gallery of changing exhibits on New York's maritime heritage.

- **Boat Building Shop**—skilled craftsmen restoring a pilot's gig and a single-masted sandbagger.

- **Pilothouse**—from a 1923 New York Central tugboat.

- **Container Store**—children's gifts and souvenirs with a nautical flair.

- **Maritime Crafts Center**—carvers, painters, and craftsmen at work on models, ship carvings, and figureheads, and delighting seafarers and landlubbers alike with stories of a bygone era.

- **Fulton Fish Market**—the largest wholesale fish market in America comes alive while New York sleeps. Tours at dawn from spring through fall.

- **Museum Shop**—ship models, toys, kites—souvenirs of the seaport.

146 Gateway to America

SOUTH STREET SEAPORT
The public visits one of the many sailboats docking at Pier 17.

Historic Ships

Climb aboard the *Peking*, a landmark of the Seaport. This four-masted, 347-foot bark is the second-largest sailing ship in existence today.

Stroll the decks of the sidewheeler *Andrew Fletcher* or the recreated, turn-of-the-century steamboat *De Witt Clinton* and witness the dramatic beauty of Miss Liberty and other enchanting harbor sites.

Step aboard *Pioneer* for a two- or three-hour sail into New York's past. Join in raising the sails or take the helm and feel the century-old schooner respond to the wind.

The *Ambrose* is New York Harbor's famed red lightship that once guided ships to port.

The *W. O. Decker* is a little wooden tugboat that could have been the model for the children's classic, "Little Toot."

The *Wavertree* is a magnificent three-masted tall ship built in England in 1885.

The *Major General William H. Hart* is a 1925 steam ferry that once carried commuters to and from Manhattan Island.

The *Lettie G. Howard* is reminiscent of the clipper-bowed schooners that once filled the Fish Market slips with their cargoes.

The *Clearwater*, a 106-foot-long sloop launched by folk singer Pete Seeger in the 1960s, is a constant reminder of the need to protect metropolitan waterways from pollution. Each year the *Clearwater* celebrates the Hudson River Revival with a sparkling sea of entertainment: jazz, blues, country, gospel, folk, storytelling, crafts, jugglers, ethnic foods, and new vaudeville. The *Clearwater* is a frequent guest at the South Street Seaport.

Rounding out the busy Seaport schedule is a new concept in New York harbor sailing—the Manhattan Yacht Club, offering corporate and individual membership that provides easy reserved sailing and racing on a fleet of J-24s.

The Marketplace

The Marketplace features six special places of interest, beginning with Cannon's Walk Block, a block of 19th and 20th century structures filled with shops, restaurants, outdoor cafes, a theater, and a courtyard.

The Fulton Market Building reflects the 1883 food market for New York City—an atrium with three floors of food markets, eateries, "Topside Shops and Cafes," several fine restaurants, the Beekinan Market seasonal pushcarts, and the Museum's Small Craft Collection.

The Pier 17 Pavilion is modeled after the immense recreation piers of yesteryear. Pier 17 overlooks the harbor and the historic tall ships. Its three floors are loaded with shops, specialty stores, food stalls, the seasonal pushcarts, and a variety of restaurants.

Schermerhorn Row embraces the sloping roofs and tall chimneys of early 19th century edifices, forming the architectural centerpiece of the Seaport. Built on speculation by Peter Schermerhorn, the block contains a pub, restaurant, and several specialty stores.

SOUTH STREET SEAPORT
South Street Seaport ice skating rink.

One Seaport Plaza is a tall, modern office building standing in striking contrast to its smaller 19th century neighbors. The Plaza offers fine stores, shops, and a café at street level.

The Shops on Front Street occupy 19th and 20th century buildings lining the street and housing a collection of splendid galleries and shops.

Dining, especially, is a delicious experience at the South Street Seaport. Visitors may choose from sumptuous banquets, buffets, and brunches of the freshest seafood and steaks served on elegant white tablecloths overlooking the harbor, to casual dining on crab sandwiches and pizza, to eating "alfresco" and the relaxing pastime of people-watching.

Among the many places to eat and feast are Boardwalk Cafe, Cafe Cafe, Container Cafe, Diner Dogs, Fluties Pier 17, Fulton Street Cafe, Fulton Market Raw Bar, The Grill, Harbour Lights, Jade Sea, Liberty's Oyster Bar, Liberty Cafe, MacMenanlin's Irish Pub, McDuffee's Irish Coffee House, North Star Pub, Pastrami Factory, Pedro O'Hara's, Pizza on the Pier, Publicans on the Pier, Roebling's (the Roeblings built the Brooklyn Bridge), Salad Bowl, Sloppy Loule's, Sweet's, Wok and Roll, and the Yankee Clipper.

Directions

At the southern tip of Manhattan Island.

Bibliography

South Street Seaport brochure.

Broadside, South Street Seaport Museum, members' calendar of events and programs, autumn, 1989.

Seaport, New York's History Magazine, summer 1989.

Chapter 9

Newport

Its shining towers complementing the sparkling skyscrapers of Battery Park City, Newport on the New Jersey side of the Hudson River is yet another stunning example of a wasted waterfront magically being transformed into a modern urban miracle.

This 21st century, $10 billion marine mecca is home to more than 30,000 residents. It was developed by the Lefrak Organization, the same company that developed Battery Park City in the 1980s, Lefrak City in the 1960s, and Kings Bay Housing in the 1950s.

Newport, the newest "Miracle on the Hudson," is a self-contained waterfront mosaic of arcades, museums, theaters, parks, playgrounds, greenways, shopping malls, elegant residential towers, luxurious hotels, entertainment piers, marinas, a yacht club, an oceanographic center, a convention-conference center, a health/fitness center; and a six-mile long riverfront esplanade.

All of this—and more—with sweeping, breathtaking vistas of the Manhattan skyline, the river, and harbor; the Statue of

NEWPORT
The view of Newport City from Manhattan.

Liberty, and the gleaming arches of the George Washington and Verrazano Bridges.

Designed by America's foremost architects and planners, Newport is the quintessential environment in which to live, work, shop, and play—the ultimate 21st-century city on the historic Hudson waterway.

The 600-acre waterfront site in Jersey City shares much of America's heritage since precolonial times. It was first sighted by Henry Hudson in 1609 when he sailed in his *Half Moon* up the river that now bears his name. It's where Dutch farmers first settled the land along this wondrous swath of water then teeming with fin and shellfish. It was the scene of early Colonial trade and the Revolutionary War armies on their way to victory ... George Washington, Alexander Hamilton, Robert Fulton and his steamboat ... transcontinental railroads reaching out to Western horizons and delivering America's bounty to Eastern shores ... immigrants savoring their first sights of America ...

Liberty ships making the world "Safe for Democracy" in two World Wars …

These are all part of the intrinsic old world values enriching Newport's equally historic and futuristic ambiance.

Enter the new world of the James Monroe luxury condominium via a cul-de-sac whose gatehouse provides around-the-clock security. A meticulously landscaped plaza and magnificent two-story lobby greet residents and their guests.

A total of 9,000 high-rise residences make up Newport's living community, including the 755-unit Towers of America condominium.

There is the 14-story, 455,000-square-foot Newport Center I occupied by Recruit U.S.A., representing the largest office lease undertaken by a Japanese corporation doing business in the U.S. A computer services corporation based in Tokyo, Recruit employs more than 1,000 people at Newport Center I. The office lobby is enhanced by two murals, each 15 x 45 feet,

NEWPORT
Newport Waterfront Marina on the Hudson River.

NEWPORT
The view of the pre-9/11 Manhattan skyline from Newport Marina.

depicting scenes from Newport's incredible history of a new nation's beginnings and struggle for freedom and independence.

Newport Tower, at 36 stories, is New Jersey's tallest building. The major tenant in this million-square-foot structure is The Limited, Inc., which occupies 400,000 square feet. The Tower connects with Newport Mall, the Pavonia-Newport Subway Station, and a light-rail station.

Newport Office Park, comprising 4.2 million square feet, is one of the metropolitan region's finest commercial complexes.

The 1.2 million-square-foot Newport Center is an enclosed three-story shopping mall anchored by Sears, Stern's, and J.C. Penney, with 110 additional stores, 20 restaurants, and nine movie theaters. Parking is available for up to 5,000 cars.

Newport Plaza, a 150,000-square-foot convenience shopping strip in the northwest section, is home to New Jersey's first Waldbaum's, which occupies 55,000 square feet.

The Newport Swim and Fitness Center contains an Olympic-sized, climate-controlled swimming pool, sun decks, saunas, whirlpools, state-of-the-art exercise equipment, and aerobics rooms. Next to the Fitness Center is a tennis facility with four all-weather courts and a tennis pro.

The Newport Marina contains 1,000 boating slips and a Yacht Club.

An on-site heliport offers both passenger and emergency services. There is on-site ingress and egress to the PATH train system connecting Newark and Jersey City to the World Trade Center site and Pennsylvania Station in Manhattan, as well as road connections to the Holland Tunnel, Pulaski Skyway, New Jersey Turnpike, and U.S. Routes 1 and 9, all offering a wide variety of travel alternatives.

Newark International Airport is just 15 minutes away.

Directions

To reach the Jersey City Hudson River waterfront, facing Manhattan, take the New Jersey Turnpike to Exit 14-C (Holland Tunnel).

Chapter 10

Gateway National Recreation Area

Within an hour's reach of 25 million metropolitan denizens is a more than 26,000 acre urban paradise of beaches and bays, dunes and marshes, forests and grasslands, trails and coves, wildlife habitats and historic sites.

Here, one can escape into a variegated marine world of swimming and fishing, boating and hiking, strolling and playing, exploring and learning, viewing and resting.

Welcome to the Gateway National Recreation Area—the great peoples' park in the New York and New Jersey harbor!

Gateway is the first and largest recreation retreat of its kind in the United States. That this unique environment has been preserved in the midst of the biggest megalopolis in the world is the result of both technological change and citizens' determination to save green open space in the most crowded corridor on the planet.

New York and New Jersey started offering the Gateway lands as a public trust in the late 1960s. In 1969, then U.S. Interior Secretary Walter Hickel, a former Governor of Alaska, proposed the Gateway plan. The United States Congress responded in

1972 by enacting legislation that created the Gateway National Recreation Area. The National Park Service was given the responsibility of managing these long-neglected natural resources and implementing a $300 million improvement program.

At the entrance to the heavily developed New York-New Jersey estuary, Gateway embraces two arms of land stretching across tidal waters toward each other, forming a natural gateway to America's busiest port. This is the legendary entrance through which some 17 million immigrants entered the New World—the gateway which has given its name to an incredible national park site.

One of these protruding land arms on the northern New Jersey shore is Sandy Hook—home of the oldest operating lighthouse in the United States.

The other arm is the Rockaway peninsula in New York, site of Breezy Point.

Lying within these outstretched arms of salty sand are the other two units of the Gateway park system—Jamaica Bay and the Staten Island bayfront.

Wandering through Gateway, one can imagine what the land was like when European settlers arrived here in the 1600s. Over the centuries, the land and water have been drastically altered by humans and their technology. Algonquin Indian encampments and villages numbering around 100 eventually gave way to farms, forts, warehouses, and mills powered by the wind and tides. As the New York-New Jersey harbor region grew, docks were built along the shores and wetlands were filled so they could support roads, houses, factories, and, later, railroads and airports. Many birds and marine animals disappeared. The waters turned foul from the effluent of manufacturing plants and the air became polluted from smokestack industries. Fish populations declined and economically vital oyster and clamming industries shut down when these shell species were no longer fit for human consumption.

Some waters were unsafe and off-limits for swimming. By the 1950s, a dark cloud had settled over Gateway's troubled waters and the shores they touched. The precious Gateway environment had been degraded, overused, and radically altered by careless development and unchecked pollution.

But love for the natural world and healthy outdoor recreation would not die. In 1953, a man-made wildlife refuge was established in Jamaica Bay through the efforts of master builder Robert Moses and developed through the dedication of horticulturist Herbert Johnson.

At Sandy Hook, the rare holly forest was preserved through careful management by the New Jersey Park Commission. In New York's Rockaways, concerned citizens halted the building of a high-rise complex to preserve the natural quality of a special stretch of ocean beach.

Then, in the late 1960s, came a nationwide clamor for cleaner air, clear water, and the preservation of natural beauty and open spaces long overlooked in the Gateway.

This new consciousness at both the local and national levels resulted in two related efforts: restoring the quality of the metropolitan environment and establishing Gateway's character.

Since the Gateway National Recreation Area opened in 1974, there has been a continuing cleanup of the waterways and beaches and millions of people now enjoy the Gateway experience each year.

When improvements are completed, Gateway will serve more visitors than any other park in the nation.

The four separate units of Gateway offer many kinds of active and leisurely recreation and countless ways to explore the natural environment and historic sites. The National Park Service continuously changes and expands its programs and experiments to meet the needs of its vast and varied audience.

Sandy Hook

Jutting out into the Gateway bay like a spit of sand is a 6.5-mile-long peninsula at the tip of the northern Jersey shore named for its natural and rather appropriate nautical shape—Sandy Hook (Exit 117 off the Garden State Parkway).

Ending New Jersey's Atlantic shoreline, Sandy Hook covers approximately 1,665 land acres, including 7.5 miles of ocean

SANDY HOOK—FORTIFICATIONS
Ancient fortifications at Fort Hancock, Sandy Hook.

beaches and sheltered bayside coves called Horse Shoe and Spermaceti.

Sandy Hook is an exciting mix of tidal niches, dunes, beaches, "heathlands," and a more than 300-year-old holly forest unsurpassed on the eastern seaboard. Some 300 migratory birds on the Atlantic Flyway, as well as year-round waterfowl, seek food and shelter on this tidal beachhead, including the endangered osprey.

Because of its attraction to residents of nearby North Jersey and New York City, one of the first stations of the U.S. Lifesaving Service was established at Sandy Hook in the late 1800s.

At the northern end, the "eternal beacon" stands solid and erect as the oldest operating lighthouse in America. The original lighthouse was erected in 1764, a decade before the stirrings of a colonial revolt.

Nearby, Fort Hancock represents more than 200 major and minor military-support structures dating back to before the

SANDY HOOK
America's oldest operating lighthouse in Sandy Hook, New Jersey, part of the Gateway National Recreation Area.

SANDY HOOK—FORT HANCOCK
World War II fortifications.

Spanish-American War. Ancient gun batteries, buried in and around the dunes throughout "The Hook," are of considerable historical and visual interest.

At one time during the Cold War period, Fort Hancock served as a Nike missile base. All but one of the missiles have been removed, the last remaining as a harmless museum piece depicting America's entry into the nuclear age.

Today, the fort is the center of activity as "Gateway Village." The proof battery, Officers' Club, and other buildings have been restored. A full range of year-round activities are available to visitors, including environmental and historical programs, cultural events, workshops in various crafts, art and puppet shows, and athletic events and programs.

Tours of Fort Hancock and areas such as the holly forest are offered daily during the summer as are lifesaving demonstrations and presentations about early lifesaving methods and puppet shows for the young. The Fort Hancock post theater, or auditorium, presents lectures and special performances. Educational field trips and workshops for teachers and classes

Gateway National Recreation Area 163

JACOB RIIS PARK
One of the two towers at the famous bathhouse at Jacob Riis Park in the Rockaways, New York.

JACOB RIIS PARK
Detail of Jacob Riis Park Landmark bathhouse.

are programmed throughout the year. Four campsites are available to youth groups by reservation.

Sandy Hook is also the site of an $18 million Marine Science Laboratory. The sundry laboratories are used by marine scientists from the U.S. National Oceanic & Atmospheric Administration (NOAA), which occupies 35,000 square feet of lab and office space. The New Jersey Department of Environmental Protection (DEP) has another 20,000 square feet for researchers, faculty members, and students from the state's colleges and universities.

The Hook is the home of the New Jersey Marine Sciences Consortium, and the American Littoral Society, a national marine conservation organization.

Breezy Point

This unit of Gateway, lying south of Jamaica Bay on the western end of the Rockaway peninsula, takes in about 1,100

Gateway National Recreation Area 165

JACOB RIIS PARK
Jacob Riis Park landmark outdoor clock.

acres and 4.5 miles of beaches. The popular Jacob Riis Park, established by New York City during the 1930s Depression period, and the Fort Tilden military complex are the main attractions on Breezy Point, so-named because of the fresh salty air blowing in from the Atlantic Ocean.

The vegetation on the undisturbed areas within Breezy Point is typical of barrier beaches in the mid-Atlantic region. At the western end, "The Tip," some 200 acres of sand dunes, salt marshes, brackish marshes, and grasslands remain in a relatively undisturbed condition.

The Fort Tilden area contains beachgrass dunes, grasslands, phragmites, high and low thickets, and coniferous and deciduous forests at higher elevations where the dunes have stabilized.

Adjacent to Riis Park, the Army fort possesses a mixture of quasi-natural areas and assorted military structures from several historic periods. A narrow one-mile-long beach stretches from in front of the fort complex, backed by a narrow primary dune system.

Two clubs are open for membership on a first-come, first-served basis.

The Silver Gull Beach Club, occupying a portion of the shorefront at Tankel Beach, offers a variety of recreational facilities, ranging from two cabanas; three swimming pools; an assortment of tennis, basketball, paddle tennis, and volleyball courts; and a restaurant and bar.

The Breezy Point Surf Club occupies a site near the beach at the "Tip" of Breezy Point. Among the amenities are a cafeteria, restaurant, bar, two swimming pools, field and court areas, and a surrounding trail system extending to the beach and jetty to provide access for fishing and surfing.

From early spring through fall, National Park Rangers lead thousands of school children through explorations along ocean and bay beaches to discover the fascinating world of marine life. Fort Tilden, a defense point for New York City intermittently since the War of 1812, becomes a site for supervised school camping during the week, and on weekends offers the general public "Photo Safari" tours of the Fort's dune areas, as well as classes in crafts using the natural materials and patterns of the marine ecosystem. Special programs are available to groups on request about the history of the Rockaway peninsula.

Summer programs at Breezy Point include visits by organized groups of young people and senior citizens to Fort Tilden for games, picnicking, swimming, gardening, environmental education, and crafts. Fall and spring bring to the Mall at Riis Park such special events as craft shows and theatrical performances.

Jamaica Bay

This Gateway unit encompasses about 4,450 acres of land and marshes in and near Jamaica Bay.

The Jamaica Bay Wildlife Refuge includes 2,474 acres of uplands and low-lying islands surrounded by saltwater, freshwater, and brackish impoundments. Two artificially created ponds—the brackish East Pond and the freshwater West Pond—increase the variety of habitats available to more than 300 species of birds either residing in or migrating through the refuge.

The coastal shoals, bars, and mud flats in Jamaica Bay provide habitat for a number of invertebrates and birds. Extensive Spartina salt marshes surround most of the islands and land masses in and around the bay.

Among the hundreds of bird species utilizing the salt marshes are the glossy ibis, the great blue heron, the snowy egret, the marsh hawk, the clapper rail, the eastern kingbird, and a variety of gulls.

Nesting sites for common terns, herring gulls, snowy and cattle egrets, and great black-backed gulls are commonly observed in Jamaica Bay.

The refuge is most exciting during the spring nesting season and the fall migration when thousands of ducks and geese on the Atlantic Flyway stop over on the two refuge ponds. During these seasons the refuge provides weekday morning programs for school classes and programs for the general public in the afternoon and on weekends.

Guided "Explore the Beach" programs are offered at North Channel, Dead Horse Bay, and Plumb Beach to school classes during the spring and fall and to the general public during the summer. A summer Crafts Mobile brings free instruction to Plumb Beach and Canarsie Pier, as well as to Frank Charles Park.

One of the largest segments of the Jamaica Bay national recreation area is Floyd Bennett Field, a former Naval air base. This 1,448-acre blend of open space and aging facilities was New York's first municipal airport. Though it did not succeed commercially, it contributed to the development of aviation as the takeoff point for many record-breaking flights by such pilots as aviation pioneer and Hollywood producer Howard Hughes, Wiley Post, Laura Ingalls, Colonel Roscoe Turner, "Wrongway" Corrigan, and astronaut John Glenn. Floyd Bennett Field currently offers programs for teachers and school children through the Gateway Environmental Study Center, which is run cooperatively with the New York City Board of Education, as well as a demonstration of community gardening and recreation programs for organized groups.

The previously established golf, tennis, and marina facilities at Dead Horse Bay remain popular attractions. Canarsie Pier features a promenade, a concession stand, and public lavatories. The Frank Charles and Hamilton Beach Parks, bordered by fringe salt marshes, provide playgrounds, ballfields, tennis courts, and picnic grounds.

Staten Island

The fourth component of the Gateway National Recreation Area extends along the southeastern shore of Staten Island off the Staten Island Expressway. It includes (from south to north) Great Kills Park, Oakwood and New Dorp Beaches, Miller Field, Midland and South Beaches, historic Fort Wadsworth, and two small man-made islands—Hoffman and Swinburne—lying just offshore. Collectively these tracts total 1,120 acres along a 7.5-mile long beachfront.

Fort Wadsworth is the site of another Gateway Village. The fort's history as a strategic military installation goes back before the Revolutionary War. The fort contains many interesting examples of late 19th century military architecture. The fort's oceanfront development consists of several old structures of major historic significance, including Battery Weed and a number of heavy gun emplacements. Battery Weed and Fort Tompkins, another important military structure, are listed on the National Register of Historic Places.

Hoffman and Swinburne Islands were constructed in the 1870s for use as quarantine stations. Their buildings were disused and abandoned in the 20th century.

Swimming and fishing are centered at Great Kills Park in the usually calm waters of Lower New York and Raritan bays. Great Kills facilities include football and baseball fields and a former bathhouse with rooms now used for community meetings (by reservation) and for environmental education. To the northeast of the bathhouse, a peat bog reaches into the bay.

The upland core of Great Kills Park is used primarily for organized activities such as model airplane flying and field games. Some nature study also takes place.

Environmental field trips are available to school classes and organized groups during the spring and fall, and specially scheduled bird walks, geology walks, Monarch butterfly walks, and star watches are then offered for the general public.

During the summer, there are discovery walks over woodland, grassland, dune, and beach trails for both organized groups and drop-in visitors.

The center of Crooke's Point is being allowed to return to a natural state and will be preserved as a habitat for plants, birds, and rabbits, as well as one of the Staten Island stopping-places for Monarch butterflies in their annual migration to and from Mexico.

The early hangar complex at Miller Field is being preserved and made available for adaptive public use. Miller Field is dedicated to ballgames of all kinds; it has six tennis courts and a roller hockey rink.

Directions

From New York or New Jersey, take the Staten Island Expressway via the Verrazano Bridge or the Outer Bridge from the New Jersey Turnpike or Garden State Parkway

Bibliography

GATEWAY GENERAL MANAGEMENT PLAN, Gateway National Recreation Area, New York/New Jersey, United States Department of the Interior National Park Service, August 1979.

GATEWAY color brochure, National Recreation Area, New York/New Jersey, National Park Service, U.S. Department of the Interior, 1989.

"GATEWAY: Where the City Meets the Sea," Friends of Gateway, 51 Chambers Street, New York, NY 10007, and the J.M. Kaplan Fund, NY, 1989.

"Marine Sciences Lab," by Bill Gannon, *The Star-Ledger*, Newark, NJ, October 12, 1989.

About the Author

Gordon Bishop, a national award-winning author, historian, and syndicated columnist, is the recipient of eight Congressional Commendations, 12 National Journalism Awards, and 15 State Journalism Awards, including a Pulitzer finalist in 1971 and New Jersey's first "Journalist of the Year"—1986/New Jersey Press Association.

Mr. Bishop, a native of Hackensack, New Jersey, is the unprecedented five-time consecutive winner (1971–1975) of the Scripps-Howard Foundation's National Journalism Award in Conservation Writing, and the unprecedented four-time winner of the New Jersey Society of Professional Journalists' (Sigma Delta Chi) Distinguished Public Service Award.

He is the author of seven books and has published more than 10,000 by-line articles, columns, and editorials for *The Newark Star-Ledger* (1969–1996) and *The North Jersey Herald-News* (1959–1968). He was inducted into the Literary Hall of Fame in 1988 and hosted a weekly television show, *New Jersey Issues*, from 1988 to 1996. His weekly syndicated column is "Gordon Bishop on the Issues."

Since the 1970s, Mr. Bishop has written, produced, and narrated a dozen documentaries for PBS, NJN (New Jersey Network), and CTN (Cable Television Network) through his nonprofit company, Bishop Public Programs, Inc., Eatontown, New Jersey.

About the Photographer

Jerzy Koss, architect, artist, and photographer, is a Polish-born immigrant who holds a master's degree in Architecture and Urban Planning from the University of Gdansk, Poland. He left Poland in 1965 and came to the United States in 1967. From 1965 to 1972 he worked as an architectural designer and urban planner in Paris, France; Montreal, Canada; Cleveland, Ohio; and New York City, where he has resided on Fifth Avenue since 1969. Here he has a perfect view of his favored photo subject, the famous Flatiron Building. For 35 years he has been involved with a wide range of photographic activities including News Photography of world leaders, Prime Ministers, and Presidents, from the White House Oval Office, United Nations Secretaries General, UN General Assembly and Security Council, to the Vatican and international events.

In 1971 Jerzy founded the Koss Family Artists, exhibiting his artwork worldwide for 31 years. His artwork has reached millions through television, film newsreels, radio, press, private and public collections, books, and Internet Web sites. His numerous monumental exhibits include: Vatican exhibit viewed by Pope John Paul II; New York City exhibits: Rockefeller Center, World Trade Center (entire Lobby Mezzanine, North Tower and Main Lobby of South Tower); Park Avenue Atrium, 55 Water Street, World Financial Center; Richard J. Daley Civic Center in Chicago; Peace Exhibit (60,000 square feet) in Cairo, Egypt at the invitation of president Anwar Sadat; Peace Exhibits in Poland: Warsaw, Krakow, Wroclaw, Gdansk (exhibit opened with participation of Lech Walesa, Nobel Peace laureate, Solidarity leader, president of Poland); retrospective museum exhibit at Butler Institute of American Art celebrating Centennial of Statue of Liberty.

Koss was interviewed, published, or featured in such national and international mass media as the *New York Times*, *USA Today*, *Christian Science Monitor*, *Art Gallery Magazine*, *Architectural Record*, *Oggi Magazine* (Italian), *Osservatore Romano* (Vatican); international press agencies including Reuters, AP, UPI, Canadian Press, Agence France Presse, ANSA (Italian), Kyodo (Japanese), Middle East News Agency; many television programs, among them *CBS Evening News*, *CNN News*, *ABC News*, *NBC News*, Channel 13, ARD German-TV (documentary film), Tokyo Broadcasting System, and countless other TV programs including the U.S., Germany, Italy, Poland, Egypt, and other countries. Koss is co-founder and past president of the Polish Photographic Club of New York. He is listed in Who's Who in Polish America.

Index

A

Adams, Christy Cunningham, 67
Albany, New York, 106
Algonquin, 158
Allen, Debbie, 38
Allied Forces, 76
Ambrose, 147
American Bicentennial, 55
American Express, 131–132
American Littoral Society, 91, 164
American Museum of Immigration, 21
American Revolution (*see* Revolutionary War)
Amherst, Lord Jeffrey, 101
Ammann & Whitney, 33
Andrew Fletcher, 147
Anglo-Dutch War, 99
Angola, 109
Appalachian mountains, 113
Arlington National Cemetery, 84
Arm & Hammer, 36
Atlantic Flyway, 160, 167
Atlantic Ocean, 166
aviation, 106

B

Baltimore and Ohio Railroad, 75
Bard, John, 18
Bardin, David J., 80–82
Barge Office, 44
Bartholdi, Frederic August, 16, 18–20, 23, 25, 33, 35
Baryshnikov, Mikhail, 38
Basel Ballet, 132
Battery Park City, 1, 104, 118, 124, 127–140, 151
    Arc, 134
    architecture, 128, 131
    Esplanade, 132, 134, 140
    Liberty Street, 134
    Master Plan, 129–131
    Plaza, 132–134, 137
    Rector Park, 137, 139–140
    Rector Place, 137
    sculpture, *133*
    Summer Park, 134
    urban design and planning, 127–132
    West Park, 134
    Winter Garden, 131, 137
    World Financial Center, 128, 131–132, 137
Battery Park City Authority, 129

Battery Weed, 169
Battle of Fort Erie, 18
Bayonne, 3, 77, 90
Bedloe, Isaac, 16
Bedloe's Island, 16, 23, 42–43
Beekinan Market, 148
Bergen County, 7
Berlin, Irving, 38
Black Tom Wharf, 46, 76
Boat Building Shop, 145
Bolsheviks, 46
Book & Chart Store, 144
Borglum, Gutzon, 30
Bowne & Co., Stationers, 143
Breezy Point, 158, 164–167
    dune areas, 166
    military structures, 166
    natural areas, 166
    Silver Gull Beach Club, 166
    Tankel Beach, 166
Briganti, Stephen, 65
Brooklyn Bridge, 99, 141
Brooklyn Philharmonic, 132
Brooklyn, 3, 99–100, 106
Buchewald Concentration Camp, 85
Buckley, Kevin, *34*, 69
Bureau of Immigration, 44
Bush, George, 110
Buttermilk Channel, 100, 106
Byrne, Brendan, 78–81

C

C. Washington Coyler, 55
Cahill, William, 78, 123
Cakapeteyno, 97
Calder, Alexander, 116
Caldwell, New Jersey, 23

Cannon's Walk Block, 148
Castle Clinton, 42, 104
Castle Garden, 43
Castle Williams, 42, 103, *104*
Caven Point, 91
Center for Housing Partnerships of New York, 60
Central Railroad of New Jersey, 74–77
Central Railroad Terminal, 75–76, 82, 92, 94
Chapel of Saint Cornelius the Centurion, 107
Charles II, 7–8
China Science and Technologies Exchange Center, 124
cholera, 68
Chrysler, 1, 59
Circle Line ferry, *66*, 82
City University of New York, 111
Civil War, 43, 74, 103–104
Clearwater, 147
Cleveland, Grover, 23, 68
coal, 74
Coast Guard Support Center, 107, *108*
Cohen, Edward, 33
Cold War, 162
Coleman, John, 4
Commissioned Corps of the Marine Hospital Service, 68
Commodity Exchange, 123
Communipaw, 75, 92
Communist organizations, 47
Connecticut River, 7
Cooper, Alexander, 129
Copeland, Aaron, 38
Cornbury, Lord, 100
Corrigan, "Wrongway," 168
Cuba, 109
Curiosity Shop, 144
Curtis, Glen, 106

D

da Verrazano, Giovanni, 1–3, 97
de Vauban, Sebastien, 103
De Witt Clinton, 147
Delaware Bay, 7
Delaware River, 74
Department of Environmental Protection (*see* New Jersey Department of Environmental Protection)
Diamond, Neil, 38
Doak, William N., 47
Dow Jones, 131
Downtown Lower Manhattan Association, 117
Dutch colony, 3, 4, 7, 41, 73–74, 97–99, 152
Dutch East India Company, 3
Dutch House, 106

E

Eagle, 17, 59
Earth Day, 52, 77
East Gibson, 42
East River, 1, 128, 141
Eckstut, Stanton, 129
economy, 2
Edison, Thomas Alva, 20
Eiffel Tower, 23
Eiffel, Alexandre Gustave, 20, 23, 33
Elizabeth and Somerville Railroad Company, 74
Elizabeth, NJ, 75
Ellis Island, 2, 7, 11, 38, 41–70, 90, 104, 141
    architecture, 45
    American immigrant Wall of Honor, 64
    Baggage Room, 63
    centennial, 61
    decline of, 47–48
    fire of 1897, 44
    graffiti messages, 67
    Great Hall, 62–64, 68
    immigration depot, 43
    "Isle of Tears," 45–47
    Main Hall, 62
    Main Registry Building, 66
    "melting pot," 48–50
    restoration, *50*, 50–61
    study areas, 64
Ellis Island Immigration Center, 6, *50*, 75
Ellis Island Immigration Museum, 62
Ellis, Samuel, 42
Emery Roth and Sons, 118
Empire State Building, 1
English colony, 5, 7–8, 74, 99
environmental education, 86–92, 169

F

Fairleigh Dickinson University, 51, 53
Fascist organizations, 47
Florio, James, 70, 79
Ford, Gerald, 52
Fort Columbus, 42, 103
Fort Gibson, 43–44
Fort Hancock, 160, *162*
Fort Jay, 102–103, 107
Fort Tilden, 166–167
Fort Tompkins, 169
Fort Wadsworth, 168–169

Fort Wood, 18, 42
France, 2, 14, 18
Frank, Al, 24, 29–30, 36, 57
French-American Committee for the Restoration of the Statue of Liberty, 28
French-American Union, 18, 21
French-Indian War, 101
French Revolution, 14
Fulton Fish Market, 143
Fulton Market Building, 148
Fulton, Robert, 152

G

Gallagher, Frank, 90
Garden State Parkway, 159
garment district, 1
Gates, Horatio, 101
Gateway Environmental Study Center, 168
Gateway islands, 8–10, 91, 94
Gateway National Recreation Area, 34, 157–170
General Services Administration, 48
George Washington Bridge, 152
German-Americans, 46
Gershwin, George, 38
Glenn, John, 168
Gohard, Robert and Fabrice, 31–32
Goldberger, Paul, 128
Gorbachev, Mikhail, 110
Governors Island, 7, 38, 42–43, 97–111, *99*
    aviation history, 106
    Billard Elementary School, 107

Chapel of Saint Cornelius the Centurion, 107
Child Development Center, 107
Coast Guard Special Services Division, 109
Coast Guard Support Center, 107, *108*
Dutch House, 106
Governor's House, 103
Liggett Hall, 106
lighthouse, *105*
U.S. Coast Guard, 107–109
Governor's Island Gazette, 107
Gramercy Park, 139
Graves, Michael, 86, 88–89
Great Lakes, 106

H

Half Moon, 3–4, 152
Hamilton, Alexander, 74, 102, 152
Hardenbergh, Augustus A., 43
Harding, Amanda, 39
Harrison, NJ, 124
Haworth, NJ, 39
Hayden, Richard, 27, 32, 36
Hendrickson, William, 56
Herbie Hancock Trio, 132
Hickel, Walter, 157
Hillier Group, 95
Hilton International, 116
Hitler, Adolf, 84
Hoboken, NJ, 124
Hoffman Island, 168–169
Holland Tunnel, 155
Holocaust, 84
Horsley, Carter B., 134, 137

Hudson County, NJ, 43, 75
Hudson River, 1, 5, 23, 37, 75–76, 91, 113, 118, 128–129, 137, 141, 151
Hudson, Henry, 1–4, 152
Hughes, Howard, 168
Hughes, Richard J., 78–79
Hunt, Richard Morris, 14, 19

I

Iacocca, Lee, *26*, 38, 57, 59, 70
immigrants, 2, 41, 44, 75–75, 152
immigration, 75
Immigration Act of 1891, 44
Immigration Act of 1924, 47
Immigration and Naturalization Act of 1952, 48
immigration depot, 13
Immigration Quota Law, 46
Indians (*see* Native Americans)
Industrial Revolution, 61, 74
Ingalls, Laura, 168
Internal Security Act of 1950, 47
Isere, 23
"Isle of Tears," 45–47
Italian-American, 53

J

Jacob Riis Park, *163–165*, 166
Jamaica Bay, 158–159, 164, 167–168
    aviation, 168
    Canarsie Pier, 168
    Dead Horse Bay, 167–168
    Floyd Bennett Field, 168
    Frank Charles Park, 168
    Hamilton Beach Park, 168
    North Channel, 167
    Plumb Beach, 167–168
Jamaica Bay Wildlife Refuge, 167
James, the Duke of York, 7–8
Jay, John, 103
J.C. Penney, 155
Jensen, William, 73
Jensen's Port, 92
Jersey City waterfront, 9, 46, 51, 52, 73–74, 77, 152
Jersey City, 3, 7, 20, 36, 74, 77, 124
Johnson, Herbert, 158
Johnson, Lyndon, 48
Joint Boundary Commission of New York and New Jersey, 10
Jordan, Paul T., 81

K

Kaufman, Luna, 85
Kean, Thomas, 78–79, 84
King, Coretta Scott, 38
King, Martin Luther, Jr., 38
King's Royal Rifle Corps, 106
Kings Bay Housing, 151
Kleiner, Philip, 31, 33, 35
Koenig, Fritz, 116
Koop, C. Everett, 67, 69
Kotok, David, 85

L

Laboulaye, Edouard Rene Lefebvre de, 13, 16, 18
Lautenberg, Frank R., 70
Lazarus, Emma, 13–14, 81
LeFante, Joseph A., 81

Lefrak City, 151
Lefrak Organization, 151
Lehigh Valley Railroad, 74
Leni Lenape, 4, 73, 97
Les Metalliers Champenois of
    Reims, 29
Lettie G. Howard, 147
Liberation Monument, 82–85, *84*
Liberty Harbor, 10–11, 37
Liberty Island, 7, 16, 18, 36, 90
Liberty Park Monument
    Committee, 85
Liberty State Park, *9*, 37, 55,
    73–95
        dedication, 79–82
        Environmental Education
            Center, *86*, 86–92
        Interpretive Center, 88
        Liberation Monument,
            82–85
        Liberty Science Center
            and Hall of Technology,
            93–95
        Liberty Walk, 93
        Omnitheater, 93–94
        rescue, 77–79
        time capsule, 85
Liberty State Park Development
    Corp., 92–93
Liberty Village, 109
Liberty Weekend, 37–39
lighthouse, *105*, 158, 160, 161
Limited, Inc., The, 155
Long Island, 8, 113
Lors Machinery, Inc., 33
Louis XIV, 103
Lower New York Bay, 169
Lujan, Manuel, 70

M

Maine, 7
Major General William H. Hart, 147
Manhattan Island, 1, 4, 42, 73, 82,
    99, 127, 129
Manhattan Yacht Club, 147
Manhatus, 97
marine ecosystem, 167
Marine Science Laboratory, 164
Marriott, 116
Martha's Vineyard, 8
mass transit, 124
McCabe, Jerome, 55, 78
McCann, Gerald, 70, 85
McGovern, Eugene, 25
McGreevey, James, 79
McPherson, John R., 43
"melting pot," 2, 48–50
Melville Library, 145
Merrill Lynch, 131–132
Mexican War, 103
Meyner, Robert B., 81
Minoru Yamasaki and Associates, 118
Minuit, Peter, 4
Miro, Joan, 116
Mitterand, François, 38, 109
Moffitt, David, 26–27, 58–61
Monarch butterflies, 169
Morris Canal, 74, 92
Morton, Levi, 21
Moses, Robert, 158
Mount Rushmore National
    Monument, 30
Moutard, Jacques, 27–28
Mullan, Fitzhugh, 68–69

N

NAB Construction, 33

Nagare, Masaynki, 116
Nantucket, 8
Napoleon III, 16
National Archives, 48
National Heritage Confederation, 56
National Historic Preservation Act, 60
National Park Service, 10–11, 25–27, 48, 52, 54–56, 58–61, 63, 69, 158–159
National Register of Historic Places, 169
Native Americans, 2, 4, 41–42, 73, 92, 97, 106, 158
Nevelson, Louise, 116
New Amsterdam, 4, 41, 99
"New Colossus, The," 13
New France, 106
New Jersey Department of Environmental Protection, 52, 55, 77–78, 82, 91, 164
New Jersey Marine Sciences Consortium, 164
New Jersey Park Commission, 159
New Jersey Turnpike, 94, 155
New Netherland, 3, 8, 97
New York Bight, 2
New York City Board of Education, 168
New York Coffee, Sugar, and Cocoa Exchange, 123
New York Convention Center, 1
New York Cotton Exchange, 123
New York Harbor, 1–2, 43, 79, 100, 141
New York Mercantile Exchange, 123
New York Post, 134
New York State Legislature, 129
New York Times, 128
New York Weekly Journal, 100
Newark Bay, 5
Newark International Airport, 155
Newark, NJ, 74, 124
Newhouse, S. I., Sr., 77
Newport, 151–55
　Newport Center, 1, 153, 155
　Newport Marina, *154*
　Newport Office Park, 155
　Newport Swim and Fitness Center, 155
　Newport Tower, 155
Normandy, 85
Norway Galleries, 145
Nutten Island, 97–99

O

Okanite Company, 36
Olympia & York, 131
Oppenheimer, 131
Osgood, Joseph O., 76
Owens, Jesse, 84
Oyster Islands, 8, 42

P

P.A. Fiebiger, 33
Pagganck, 97
Palatinate, 101
Palatines, 100
Palisades, 2
Park, Eleanor Irwin, 69–70
Paterson, NJ, 29, 31, 74
Paulus Hook, 74
Pavonia-Newport Subway Station, 155

Peabody and Stearns, 75
"Peace of Breda," 8
Pearl Harbor, 47
Peck, Gregory, 38
Pehiwas, 97
Peking, 147
Pelli, Cesar, 131
Pennsylvania Station, 155
Pennsylvania, 74
People's Republic of China, 124
Pepperell, Sir William, 101
Pershing, John J., 104
Pesin, Morris, 51–52, 77, 79, 82
Petronas Towers, 117
Pier 17 Pavilion, 148
Pioneer, 147
Plainfield, NJ, 84–85
pollution, 27, 147, 158–159
Port Authority Trans-Hudson (PATH) trains, 118, 124, 155
Port Authority, 5, 117, 123–124
Port District, 118
Port of New York, 2
Post, Wiley, 168
Princeton University, 88
Princeton, New Jersey, 69, 86, 95
Proclamation 3656, 48
Public Service Electric & Gas Company, 36, 92
Public Works Administration, 47
Pulaski Skyway, 155
Pulitzer, Joseph, 21, 106
Pulton Market Building, 141
Putnam, Israel, 101

Q

quarantine station, 18
Quayle, Dan, 70

R

railroad, 43, 74–77, 152, 158
Rappaport, Natan, 82–85
Raritan Bay, 4, 169
RCA, 1
Reading Railroad, 75
Reagan, Nancy, 38
Reagan, Ronald, 37–38, 57, 79, 109–110
Recruit U.S.A., 153
"Red Scare," 46
repousse, 19, 29
Restore Ellis Island Bill of 1976, 52
Restore Ellis Island Committee, 52, 54
Revenue Cutter Service, 102
Revolutionary War, 5, 8, 18, 38, 42, 74, 87, 100–103, 152, 168
Rockaway peninsula, 158–159, 164, 167
Rockefeller Center, 1, 118, 128
Rockefeller, Nelson, 118, 123, 129
Roe, Robert A., 81
Rosati, James, 116

S

Sammartino, Peter, 51–56
Sandy Hook, 3, 91, 158–164
   beaches, 160
   holly forest, 160, 162
   Horse Shoe, 160
   lifesaving, 162
   lighthouse, 160, *161*
   Marine Science Laboratory, 164
   Spermaceti, 160
   theater, 162
Sandy Hook Bay, 4

Scalia, Antonin, 70
Schermerhorn, Peter, 148
Schermerhorn Row, 148
Sears Tower, 117, 129
Sears, 155
Seeger, Pete, 147
September 11, 2001, *120–122*, 126
settlers, 2, 7
Seuner, Joseph, 44
Sheehan, Patricia Q., 81
shipping, 2, 43
Simplex Wire and Cable Company, 37
Sinatra, Frank, 38
small pox, 68
Somerville and Easton Railroad, 74
Sousa, John Philip, 38
Souter, David, 11
South Africa, 109
South Street Seaport, 1, 141–149, *142–143*
    Bowne & Co., Stationers, 143
    dining, 148
    Fulton Fish Market, 143, 147
    ice skating rink, *148*
    Manhattan Yacht Club, 147
    Marketplace, 141, 147–148
    museum, 144–145
    Pulton Market Building, 141
    ships, 147
Spanish-American War, 162
Star Ledger, 10–11, 24, 31, 52–55, 57–61, 77, 79–82, 86–92
Staten Island, 3, 100, 158, 168–169
    Crooke's Point, 169
    Great Kills Park, 168–169

Midland Beach, 168
Miller Field, 168–169
New Dorp beach, 168
Oakwood Beach, 168
South beach, 168
Staten Island Expressway, 168
Statue of Liberty, 2, 11, 13–40, 77, 86, 92, 106, 109, 141, 151
    design and construction, 16–24
    dimensions, 39–40
    Liberty Weekend, 37–39
    restoration, 24–37
Statue of Liberty-Ellis Island Foundation, 11, 24, 26–28, 57, 61, 65, 69
Statue of Liberty National Monument, 26, 48, 58
Stephens, I. J., 107
Stern's, 155
Stock Exchange, 129
stock market crash of 1929, 47
Swedish settlers, 74
Swinburne Island, 168–169

T

tall ships, *17*, 37, *142*
Taylor, Elizabeth, 38
tourism, 2
trachoma, 68–69
Treaty of Westminster (1674), 99
Trenton, New Jersey, 70
Turner, Roscoe, 168
twin towers, 129 (*see* World Trade Center)
typhus, 68

U

Udall, Stewart L., 48
Upper New York Bay, 97, 128
U.S. Army, 43, 46, 103, 107
U.S. Coast Guard, 47, 97, 102, 104, 107–109
U.S. Congress, 10, 43, 46, 157
U.S. Customs Service, 123
U.S. Department of Defense, 7
U.S. Department of the Interior, 52, 60
U.S. Department of the Treasury, 44
U.S. Department of Transportation, 102
U.S. Economic Development Administration, 124
U.S. Lifesaving Service, 160
U.S. National Oceanic & Atmospheric Administration, 164
U.S. Navy, 46, 102
U.S. Public Health Service, 67–70
U.S. Supreme Court, 11

V

Van Twiller, Wouter, 97–99
Verkuil, Paul R., 11
Verrazano Bridge, 5, 118, 152
Vienna Boys' Choir, 131
Vista International New York, 114, 123

W

Waldbaum's, 155
Wall Street, 1, 116, 131
War of 1812, 18, 42, 103, 166
Washington, George, 102, 128, 152
Waterfront photographer, 144
Wavertree, 147
Weber, John, 44
West Battery, 42
West India Company, 98
West Point Military Academy, 103
Whitman, Christine Todd, 79
Wilder, Doug, 70
Williams, Jonathan, 42, 103
Windows of the World, 114, 124
W. O. Decker, 147
Wojcicki, Walter M., 56
Wolper, David, 37
Wood, Eleazar, 18
Wood, Leonard, 106
Works Progress Administration, 47
World Financial Center, 128, 131–132, 137
World, The, 21, 106
World Trade Center, 113–126, *115*, *123*, *120*, 121, 127, 129, 131, 155
    Concourse, 114, 116
    design and construction, 117–118, 123
    "History of Trade" exhibit, 113
    International Plaza, *116*
    "King Kong Towers," 114
    Memorial Fountain, *117*
    observation deck, 113, 114, 123
    September 11, 2001, *120–122*, 126
    Skylobby, 113

Tribute in Light, *125*
Vista International New York, 117, 124
Windows of the World, 114, 123
World Trade Institute, 124
 "Export to Win," 124
 Language School, 124
World War I, 46, 76, 104
World War II, 47, 76, 84–85
Wright, Frank Lloyd, 88
Wright, Wilbur, 106

Y

yellow fever, 68

Z

Zapp, Audrey, 51–52, 55, 77, 79, 82
Zapp, Warren, 51
Zenger, John Peter, 100

More Great Books from Plexus Publishing

BOARDWALK EMPIRE
The Birth, High Times, and Corruption of Atlantic City

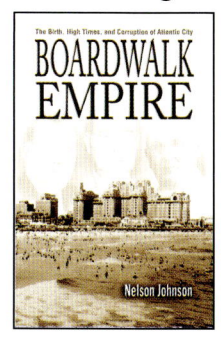

By Nelson Johnson

Atlantic City's popularity rose in the early 20th century and peaked during Prohibition. For 70 years, it was controlled by a partnership comprised of local politicians and racketeers, including Enoch "Nucky" Johnson—the second of three bosses to head the political machine that dominated city politics and society. In *Boardwalk Empire*, Atlantic City springs to life in all its garish splendor. Author Nelson Johnson traces "AC" from its birth as a quiet seaside health resort, through the notorious backroom politics and power struggles, to the city's rebirth as an entertainment and gambling mecca where anything goes.

2002/300 pp/softbound/ISBN 0-937548-49-9/$18.95

PATRIOTS, PIRATES, AND PINEYS: SIXTY WHO SHAPED NEW JERSEY

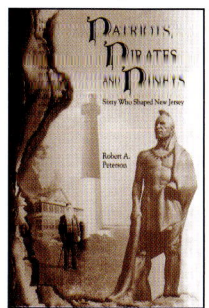

By Robert A. Peterson

"*Patriots, Pirates, and Pineys* is excellent ... the type of book that is hard to put down once you open it." —*Daybreak Newsletter*

Southern New Jersey is a region full of rich heritage, and yet it is one of the best kept historical secrets of our nation. Many famous people have lived in Southern New Jersey, and numerous world-renowned businesses were started in this area as well.

This collection of biographies provides a history of the area through the stories of such famous figures as John Wanamaker, Henry Rowan, Sara Spenser Washington, Elizabeth Haddon, Dr. James Still, and Joseph Campbell. Some were patriots, some pirates, and some Pineys, but all helped make America what it is today.

1998/155 pp/hardbound/ISBN 0-937548-37-5/$29.95
1998/155 pp/softbound/ISBN 0-937548-39-1/$19.95

THE FORKS: A BRIEF HISTORY OF THE AREA

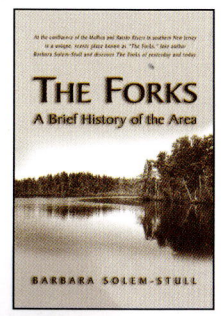

By Barbara Solem-Stull

Located on a navigable waterway, yet inland and remote, "The Forks" in South Jersey was a haven for smugglers at the dawn of the Revolutionary War. This short history describes the contribution of The Forks and its inhabitants to America's fight for independence and introduces a variety of colorful characters: early settler Eric Mullica, the treacherous Benedict Arnold, visionary citizens Elijah Clark and Richard Wescoat, ship builder Captain John Van Sant, highwayman Joe Mulliner, and the fictional Kate Aylesford—immortalized as "The Heiress of Sweetwater" in a popular novel first published in 1855.

2002/48 pp/softbound/ISBN 0-937548-51-0/$9.95

OLD AND HISTORIC CHURCHES OF NEW JERSEY, VOLUMES 1 & 2

By Ellis L. Derry

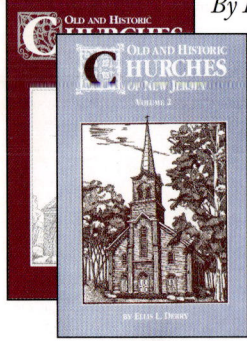

These inspirational books allow us to travel back in time to the days when this country was new—a vast and dangerous wilderness with few roads or bridges, schools or churches. It tells the stories of how our forefathers established their religious communities and houses of worship, often through great hardship and sacrifice. To be included in this two-volume history, a church had to be built by the time of the Civil War. A history of each church is given, alongside a photograph or illustration.

Vol. 1/472 pp/hardbound/ISBN 0-937548-50-2/$29.95
Vol. 1/472 pp/softbound/ISBN 0-937548-52-9/$19.95
Vol. 2/372 pp/hardbound/ISBN 0-937548-25-1/$29.95
Vol. 2/372 pp/softbound/ISBN 0-937548-26-X/$19.95

DOWN BARNEGAT BAY: A NOR'EASTER MIDNIGHT READER

By Robert Jahn

"*Down Barnegat Bay* evokes the area's romance and mystery."
—The New York Times

Down Barnegat Bay is an illustrated maritime history of the Jersey shore's Age of Sail. Originally published in 1980, this fully revised Ocean County Sesquicentennial Edition features more than 177 sepia illustrations, including 75 new images and nine maps. Jahn's engaging tribute to the region brims with first-person accounts of the people, events, and places that have come together to shape Barnegat Bay's unique place in American history.

2000/248 pp/hardbound/ISBN 0-937548-42-1/$39.95

WRONG BEACH ISLAND

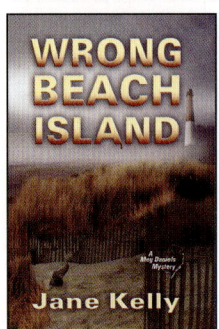

By Jane Kelly

When the body of millionaire Dallas Spenser washes up on Long Beach Island with a bullet in its back, it derails Meg Daniels's plans for a romantic sailing trip. As Meg gets involved in the unraveling mystery, she soon learns that Spenser had more skeletons than his Loveladies mansion had closets. The ensuing adventure twists and turns like a boardwalk roller coaster and involves Meg with an unforgettable cast of characters.

From the beaches of Holgate and Beach Haven at the southern end of "LBI" to the grand homes of Loveladies and the famed Barnegat Light at the north, author Jane Kelly delivers an irresistible blend of mystery and humor in *Wrong Beach Island*—her third and most deftly written novel. Meg Daniels, Kelly's reluctant heroine, may be the funniest and most original sleuth ever to kill time at the Jersey shore.

2002/327 pp/hardbound/ISBN 0-937548-47-2/$22.95

To order or for a catalog: 609-654-6500, Fax Order Service: 609-654-4309

Plexus Publishing, Inc.

143 Old Marlton Pike • Medford • NJ 08055
E-mail: info@plexuspublishing.com
www.plexuspublishing.com